"*Dig Where You Are* casts an ... ...lead-ership and driving sustainabl... ...ny kind of organization. It's an inspirational reminder of the power of purpose, conviction and customer focus."

—RICH WILLIAMS, *Chief Executive Officer, Groupon*

"*Dig Where You Are* brings to life seven individuals and the cutting edge philanthropy and social enterprise they bring to bear on a relentless societal need. None do what they do for the money, and none do it for fame; each are pulled forward by the stark need that they are uniquely qualified to fill. I urge you to read this book, then reflect on what gnarly unachievable need you are uniquely qualified to fill."

—F.K. DAY, *Founder and CEO, World Bicycle Relief and Executive Vice President, SRAM Corporation*

"Nan Doyal's book reminds us that we are not passive spectators of our own lives, our neighborhoods and communities. Today, there is no corner of the world that is not confronted by a dizzying array of challenges, large and small. Millions of thoughtful people wake up every morning caring about this, but finding themselves either frozen or overwhelmed. *Dig Where You Are* is a clarion call to action – to not waste a moment, to begin today. While there can be no assured outcomes, there is most definitely the assurance of a richer life, filled with empowerment and purpose."

—SWATI and RAMESH RAMANATHAN, *Co-Founders, JANA Group-committed to fixing India's cities*

"Nan Doyal shows us the quiet power of community-based efforts to make things better, while persuading us that we can accomplish more than we think. What is most profound is that each of the protagonists in this book has succeeded because their motivation is first and foremost to fix a problem, and not advance their own interests. It is their courage to take personal responsibility for helping others that is so inspiring and makes the message of this book an important one for us to understand and embrace, especially now."

—DANIELLE BRIAN, *Executive Director, Project on Government Oversight (POGO)*

"For more than a decade Nan Doyal helped leaders of global corporations learn from the experiences of others from different cultures and walks of life, in a unique and inspirational way. Now, as a writer she has made this opportunity available to many more. In *Dig Where You Are*, she takes us to places and people we could never find or understand on our own."

—JOHN ABRAHAMSON, *Chairman, Lund University School of Economics and Management and Managing Director, SEB*

Dig Where You Are

Dig Where You Are

How One Person's Effort Can Save a Life,
Empower a Community and Create
Meaningful Change in the World.

Nan Alexander Doyal

CASPER PRESS

Casper Press, January 2017

Published in the United States by Casper Press, Glencoe, IL
A division of The International Forum, Inc.

Library of Congress Control Number: 2016915467

Doyal, Nan Alexander
Dig where you are : how one person's effort can save
a life, empower a community and create meaningful
change in the world / by Nan Alexander Doyal –
Glencoe, Il. : Casper Press, 2017.
246 pages; 22 cm.
Includes bibliographic references
ISBN: 978-0-9973203-0-5 (Paperback)
ISBN: 978-0-9973203-1-2 (Hardcover)
1. Social justice. 2. Social change. 3. Criminals-Rehabilitation.
4. Poor-Medical care. 5. Poor-Education. 6. Low-income housing.
7. Leadership. 8. Political participation.
HM831 .D69 2017
303.4--dc21   2016915467

Book design by Sally Stetson Design

*Proceeds from the sale of this book support the efforts
of the men and women of Dig Where You Are.*

To order books in bulk contact orders@casperpress.com

2 4 6 8 10 9 7 5 3

For Brian with love,
and for Alexander and Aidan –
May you never be afraid to Dig Where You Are.

The lesson which life repeats and constantly enforces is to *"look under your foot."* You are always nearer the divine and the true sources of your power than you think. The lure of the distant and the difficult is deceptive. The great opportunity is where you are.

– JOHN BURROUGHS

Contents

Preface

For a long time I have believed in the power of human connections to help and inspire us, to give our lives purpose and meaning. But in the fall of 2007, I could no longer ignore that the connections we had historically nurtured in our societies to support one another and create shared outcomes, had either disappeared or were failing. Participation in churches, associations, community groups, and local government had been in decline for a while. Technology and social media had isolated us from each other. We were no longer engaging in each other's wellbeing to the degree we once had. There was growing skepticism and loss of trust in governments and large organizations whose job we believed was to improve conditions for more healthy and productive lives.

Yet even as our social capital seemed to be slowly eroding I was discovering pockets of hope. There were people around the world who were bringing about meaningful improvements in lives, health, and communities; and they were doing it not by delegating it to institutions but by connecting with others and finding solutions together.

Although I knew very little about social innovation at this time, I was determined to understand why and how these people had prevailed and what, if anything, they had in common. What I learned over the next several years surprised and enlightened me: None had started with a vision or a grand plan. All had simply decided to fix a problem they saw right in front of them. And in each instance, through the power of human connections something important happened.

One finds on every page a solemn warning
that society is changing shape, that mankind
lives under changing conditions,
new destinies are impending.

– ALEXIS DE TOCQUEVILLE

Introduction

In 2007, Tori Zwisler decided to plant one million trees in China. It took seven years, but when she was done, she planned for one million more. What was once desert in Inner Mongolia, a remote and sparsely populated province in China, is now a flourishing forest of 1.7 million trees that give back to the earth what was brutally taken from it after decades of exploitation.

The Million Tree Project is centered around a village whose five hundred residents remember a time when their parents tended fields of beans and millet. Desertification changed all that. Before the 1960s, the area was covered with forest. Then the trees were cleared to make way for an agricultural collective, and then the grasslands were decimated by overgrazing.

The problem is not unique. Over 30% of the land in China today is arid and unusable, and each year the desert expands a few more feet because of urbanization, damming, and deforestation. With nothing to hold it back, the dry earth is carried by the winds, creating dunes that cover more and more vulnerable land.

The purpose of the Million Tree Project was to plant enough trees to stabilize the dry earth, allowing for smaller vegetation to grow. Once the soil held, more land could be reclaimed for agriculture and plant life. Since the first million trees have been planted in Inner Mongolia, the villagers have seen a significant difference in their environment. The government has also taken notice of this relatively simple, grassroots solution that seems to be working not only to curb a long-term environmental risk, but also to improve the livelihoods and sustainability of local villagers.

Tori, a mother of two, a former businesswoman and a longtime resident of China, created the Million Tree Project as one of a number of initiatives of Shanghai Roots & Shoots. In the late 1990s, after meeting anthropologist Jane Goodall at the home of a mutual acquaintance and discussing how to engage China in the global dialogue about the future of the planet and animals, Jane convinced Tori to start a local chapter of Roots & Shoots as an associated non-government organization of the Jane Goodall Institute.

There are many Roots & Shoots chapters worldwide. Each shares a mission for positive change through education and interaction with the environment, care for animals, enhancing understanding across cultures and socioeconomic levels, and helping young people develop self-respect and confidence. But at the local level each chapter is left to innovate on its own. There were many issues to address in China, so it was up to Tori to decide where Shanghai Roots & Shoots would place its emphasis.

It is estimated that in fifteen years' time, China will have relocated about 400 million people because of infrastructure projects, the movement of jobs to urban areas, and environmental destruction. That is more than the entire population of the United States. Today more than 54% of Chinese live in cities, and that number is growing. Urbanization is also on the rise in other developing countries. The United Nations estimates that by 2030, two-thirds of the world's population will live in cities. At this rate, it won't be long before the number of people living in cities is as great as the total population of the world today. If and when that happens, what will the earth be like?

People who live in cities consume on average three times as many natural resources as their rural counterparts. In one year's time consumption of water increased by 7% in China due primarily to urban migration and increased standards of living. China is already facing water shortages. Food consumption also changes as countries urbanize and incomes increase. In South Asia cities, for example, consumption of milk and vegetables increased by 70% over a five year period, while consumption of rice declined by 4%. Similar increases were seen for eggs, fish and meat. Higher value foods that are further along the food value chain put greater demands on the natural environment.

In establishing Shanghai Roots & Shoots, Tori had no illusions about solving these big challenges. Instead, she chose to focus on something that was much harder to see: how to engage and empower the individuals in this society to come up with and be a part of long-term sustainable solutions which would ultimately benefit them all.

Shanghai Roots & Shoots is now active in almost two hundred schools and has engaged over 200,000 youth in hands-on projects in China. These youth are both highly educated and motivated, and they are teaching others what they learn. In the future, many will make up China's leadership. Tori believes that the opportunity to be a part of Roots & Shoots filled a void for them. She found the kids who joined wanted to take responsibility for something. They wanted to make things better for the future. They just hadn't had the chance yet.

"One of our projects was for kids to carry our own Roots & Shoots cloth bags instead of plastic and to tell others to do the same," she says. "Now we see people with our bags at bus stops and all over. We've already taken millions of plastic bags out of circulation in China. It's making a difference."

Other student projects have included advising local companies on how to decrease their carbon footprint; growing organic gardens and teaching others; working with migrant schools to improve access to education materials, health and nutrition information; and helping poorer communities see the benefits of implementing environmentally sustainable ways of doing things. Then, of course, there are the million trees.

Donations from both individuals and corporations fund the trees. Each costs twenty five renminbi, or about four dollars. This amount covers the purchase of the sapling, the planting of the tree, the nursery site improvement, the land preparation, and payment to the farmers.

The work is very tough. It is "man against sand," as one villager said. The weather is harsh, and when the winds blow the villagers cannot go outside. But the trees have already created a barrier to hold back the encroaching desert. In twenty years the farmers will be able to harvest what they have planted while continuing to plant more trees. They will share their profits with the local government and the forestry service.

While Tori spearheaded this idea, you will not find her listed anywhere on the Million Tree Project website. It is the students, young people, and villagers who own this. They are the ones who will see it through, live the solution, and benefit from the results long after Tori is gone.

"When altruism is depersonalized, it is not sustainable," Tori says. "When you run out of money and people aren't engaged in coming up with the solution, it is much easier for everyone to walk away. But if the effort is personalized, then people will find another way to get things done, even if they don't have any money."

I met Tori during the years I ran an organization called The International Forum. Our mission was to help business leaders to understand what was changing in the world and what that might mean for them and the companies they led. We accomplished this in part by exposing them to both unfamiliar and unexpected situations, while introducing them to people like Tori whom they would not otherwise have met.

Part of my job between 1997 and 2008 involved traveling across the world to find people who were doing interesting things and who would play a role in our programs by meeting with our group or connecting us with others. I spent time with entrepreneurs, Buddhist monks, orchestral conductors, NASA scientists, artists, rice farmers, architects, former prime ministers, factory workers, slum dwellers, doctors, and school teachers. I listened to their stories and then invited many of them to be a part of what we were doing. Almost everyone accepted. It seemed no one could resist the opportunity to meet, share, and learn from others.

During those years I met some remarkable individuals who were quietly changing their communities by solving problems that well-funded organizations and governments had not yet figured out. At first I was intrigued by how they had done this and what lessons they might impart to the leaders who attended our programs. What was it about the way they led their efforts and their people that enabled them to do what others with many more resources had not?

In 2000 we began incorporating these problem-solvers into our programs. Initially we saw that even though none were in business per se, they were providing a powerful and alternative approach to leadership that was instructive to our participants. In time we all realized that it was not just leadership they were teaching us.

Our programs explored many subjects in depth. As time went on, we noticed that one topic always generated prolonged discussion. Participants wanted to know what big things in the world would affect us all and what we were planning to do about them. For example, many of the challenges that China has been dealing with, such as the environment and urbanization, will have an effect on the rest of the world in the long term. It matters to all of us, therefore, that the Chinese are working to solve them. It also behooves us to learn from each other, for it will help us as we work on other challenges in other parts of the world. These challenges are everywhere and affect us all.

Europe has for decades been buckling under a costly social welfare system, as well as a host of social issues brought about by immigration. The arrival and settlement of millions of non-Europeans has changed the face of the continent forever. Integrating those who come from dramatically different cultures has been nearly impossible. The result has been anger, prejudice, rising unemployment, and violence. What can be done?

Meanwhile, in the U.S. the debate continues over why, in spite of spending more money per capita on healthcare and education than any other nation, a large part of the population still lags behind. Crime rates, gun violence, and urban blight are symptoms of larger and long-term societal fraying. The U.S. today imprisons at least three times more of its population than any other developed country, and the recidivism rate is more than 75%. On any given day, two million citizens are behind bars at a cost to everyone. Is there a solution?

In other parts of the world, pandemics are still claiming millions in spite of modern medicine and knowhow. Tuberculosis, for which there has been a cure for decades, is still one of the largest killers. How can this be?

If local and regional challenges are not of enough concern, the asymmetric threat of terrorism and the unpredictability of sociopathic dictators pose potential chaos for the future of world order. Some of these geopolitical challenges are best dealt with through diplomacy and by visionaries who can negotiate across interests and mobilize people to work together. But for the majority of challenges we face, it will take more than that.

The "more than that" is something we often delved into at The International Forum. Inevitably someone would ask whether the institutions we have created to deal with the big issues are up to the task. What does the future hold for organizations such as the World Bank, the World Health Organization, the Red Cross or UNICEF? Are they still capable of accomplishing what we have entrusted them to do for us? If not, what can replace them?

People with hands-on experience know that to understand problems and figure out solutions one has to be on the front line, facing the issue head on; not in an office far away from the action. Solutions rarely work the first time tried. Failures always teach us something, but only if we are present to learn from them. The best place to experience this is on the ground where the problem and the solution meet.

Unfortunately, large institutions often struggle to incorporate feedback from a distant front line. Most of these institutions find it easier for their "experts" at headquarters to develop a plan and then give it to others to implement. They also reason that putting traditional measuring standards in place from the start ensures that the process can be quickly evaluated as a success or failure. While this approach is for the most part efficient, it misses a lot. Furthermore, when things don't work, it takes much longer to find out why and even longer to adjust and try again, if at all.

In 2004, I had a conversation with a senior level person from the Red Cross. We were discussing the future of aid to the developing world. I shared with her an experience I had in Africa, where I met people who were doing work at the grassroots educating communities on AIDS, helping orphans and administering medication. They were challenged however, when they discovered that the medicine they were sent did not work unless taken on a full stomach. The people they were serving suffered from malnutrition and were too poor and weak to feed themselves. It was clear that the food issue had to be dealt with before the expensive medicine would have any effect. The international organization that had provided the medicine had no idea this was an issue; they hadn't asked. But the local groups had found ways to solve the problem through their own networks. They were able to secure a regular supply of food to patients and were thus able to make a difference between the effort succeeding or failing.

I asked the woman from the Red Cross what she thought of these small grassroots organizations that were sprouting up all over the world. Did she see an opportunity in working with them, learning about what was happening on the ground, and incorporating them into their efforts?

She acknowledged that they were well-meaning, but she felt that they were neither effective in the long term nor sustainable. They didn't have resources that are available to big aid organizations, and thus could not be counted on to supply meaningful solutions to the poor and sick. Critical mass from an experienced organization was more effective than grassroots efforts would ever be, she said. In fact, she argued, these small organizations were dangerous because they often created false hope.

When Hurricane Katrina hit New Orleans a year later, I read with interest the reports on the disappointing role that her organization had played. Even though the Red Cross arrived there early and did the best with what it had, it did not have enough basic supplies ready, and its phone lines were overloaded when people called for help. One post-mortem really caught my attention: because the Red Cross had historically been reluctant to collaborate with other nonprofit groups, church groups, and local organizations in the disaster areas before the hurricane hit, it was severely hindered in getting to the people who most needed help. Additionally, the situation revealed massive fraud in the local chapter and a loss of internal controls in the organization overall. Big was not necessarily better.

Innovation often begins with an individual and an idea, not a large institution. It then takes a few brave and creative people to embrace the idea and walk the unknown path that lies ahead. What type of person chooses this route and holds himself or herself accountable when so many others don't? Is there something we can learn from them about getting things done—important things, things that really make a difference in the world? Can they teach us how to figure out the hard stuff, how to fix the impossible problems, assuage the pain we experience, and forge the path around the things that block our way?

When I was a child my favorite bedtime story was "The Nightingale" by Hans Christian Andersen. It is the tale of a small bird and the Chinese emperor who was so moved by her song that he sought to possess her and keep her in his palace so that she would sing for him whenever he wished.

One day the Emperor of Japan gave this Chinese emperor a gift. It was a golden and jewel encrusted mechanical bird, a copy of the real nightingale. The Chinese emperor and his court came to favor this fake bird over the real one because of its physical beauty. In spite of the limited repertoire of the mechanical device, they forgot all about the real nightingale.

Upon realizing she was no longer of value to her emperor, the small live bird returned to the forest. In time the fake bird broke and could no longer sing despite countless attempts to fix it. When the emperor fell very ill, he begged for its music to drown out the rising sounds of death. But this bird would not and could not sing.

From her home in the forest, the little nightingale learned of the dire condition of her emperor, and so she returned to find him. From a branch outside his bedroom window, she sang to him throughout the night. The sweet sound of her song charmed the looming specter of Death into leaving the emperor alone. In the morning, the emperor awoke fully recovered. He was forever grateful to the little bird for saving his life.

Though I would not have known to name her as such at the time, for many years the nightingale was my hero. This tiny bird had prevailed over the monster of Death and saved her emperor. No one had expected it of her; in fact they had all but forgotten she existed. I often wondered what inspired her to come back and help the same man who had abandoned her in favor of a gilded replacement.

For more than a decade, I met many men and women who lived their lives much as the nightingale had. In small ways they had made a big difference in the world. Some had been trained for a particular vocation, others had no professional skill, and still others were illiterate. But what made them interesting to me was that they were all solving long-existing problems: criminal rehabilitation, housing for the poor, disease, affordable healthcare, the education of the underserved, and more. The world had already spent billions of dollars trying to fix these same issues, yet most remained unsolved.

In 2008, just months before the onset of the sub-prime mortgage crisis in the U.S., the run on financial markets and the ensuing bailout packages, I decided to take a leave from my job. Like many others, when the causes of the Great Recession were eventually revealed, I was appalled and disgusted at how out-of-control we had let things become. Who was minding the store?

While rapidly losing faith in the institutions that had been entrusted to do a good job for us, I began to ask myself big questions about the future. Had things spun irreversibly out of control? Was there hope? What could one person do to make a difference?

I didn't have the answers to the big questions I was asking about the future, but I knew of some men and women who did. So I set out to find several of the people I had met over the previous decade, people who were quietly changing the way things were done in the world. My purpose was to get to the root of how they had succeeded and then share what I learned with others. Telling their stories, I hoped, could teach us how to do what we do better.

My journey took me from Tori Zwisler in Shanghai, to the fields of northeast Thailand, and then to the Indian city of Bangalore; from a ghetto on the outskirts of Stockholm to the slums of Mumbai; from the remote villages of Tibet to a migrant community outside Beijing; and from the waterfront of San Francisco to gang land in North Philadelphia. I had met many problem-solvers over the years. Now I was seeking seven in particular who came from diverse socioeconomic backgrounds, cultures, religions and life experiences—people who were little known beyond their immediate communities and had used the resources on hand to accomplish what they had. Each was the antithesis of the large organization. Could they be an alternative for the future? Could they be a role model for the rest of us?

They included Mechai Viravaidya, from a privileged Thai family, who studied to be an economist, then discovered his life's mission by helping to curb the spread of AIDS to over seven million people, before reviving the economy of rural Thailand through education and entrepreneurship.

In the slums of Mumbai was Jockin Arputham, who lived on the streets for most of his life and led the urban poor in India and elsewhere in the world to find their voice. From relative obscurity, in 2014 he was nominated for the Nobel Peace Prize.

There was Nancy Harris, an American doctor, educated at Yale and Stanford, who decided to leave a career in the U.S. to fight against enormous odds in order to cure Tibetans of malnutrition and tuberculosis in the face of political and social opposition.

Lily Yeh, an American artist who was born in China and raised in Taiwan, helped to heal residents in the inner city of Philadelphia and survivors of the Rwandan genocide through art. She worked with them to rebuild their communities before returning to China to help develop a school for the children of migrant workers.

Börje Ehrstrand, an educator from the north of Finland, created a team of teachers, artists, social workers, students, parents and community leaders to rebuild a school in an immigrant ghetto outside Stockholm. The effort ultimately transformed a whole town.

In San Francisco, a criminologist and psychologist named Mimi Silbert lived alongside convicted criminals and drug addicts for over forty years and put them in charge of their own rehabilitation.

Lastly there was Devi Shetty, a heart surgeon in Bangalore, India, who was Mother Teresa's doctor before she died in Calcutta. Forever influenced by his relationship with her, he developed a way to bring first-class healthcare to over three million of India's poorest in less than a decade.

I had not seen some of these people for several years. I worried they might not remember me. But I need not have been concerned. Each welcomed me, brought me to their communities, into their homes, and introduced me to their families. As I reconnected with them, I was struck by how ordinary they all were; they could have been any of us. I was also intrigued by their apparent selflessness. More important than their own success was how they affected the lives of people around them. They reaffirmed for me that the worth of a life is not measured by how much we achieve; rather it is derived from the nature of our relationships with others. At a time when I had begun to lose faith, they helped me to understand how big solutions don't solve big problems—individuals do—and that those of whom we expect the least often have the most to contribute.

The Alchemist

Each man has only one genuine vocation—
to find the way to himself...his task is
to discover his own destiny—not an arbitrary one—
and live it wholly and resolutely within himself.

– HERMAN HESSE

Lily Yeh

The columns of red flowers that flank the metal gate look as if they are painted on, but if you touch them you'll feel edges under your fingers tips. Thousands of tiny pieces of white, red, blue, green and brown ceramic shards have been cut or deliberately broken from old tile and arranged in mosaics. A blue sky holds up yellow stars, while pink petal flowers spin in the air. Clouds curl above the gate like those in Van Gogh's *Starry Night*. Here, in a dusty village on the outskirts of Beijing, an old abandoned factory has been transformed into a piece of art and with it the lives of hundreds of children from China's floating migrant population.

Lily Yeh, the artist responsible for this, stands in front of the gate. She has already called to let one of the teachers know she has arrived. She waits to be let inside. Her small figure is cloaked in a brown tunic of African batik. A strand of carefully chosen earthen beads hangs around her neck. Her dark hair is cut neat and short;

her coal black eyes are framed by large round sunglasses.

Thirty years ago, Lily was a studio artist and a professor of fine arts in Philadelphia. But in 1986, when a man invited her to create an art park in a vacant lot in one of the toughest neighborhoods in the United States, she had no idea that by saying yes to him she would change the course of her life forever. Nor could she have guessed that this project in North Philadelphia would lead her to work in the slums of Africa, Latin America, and then here to Shou Bao Zhuang, a small community in the Daxing District of China's capital city.

The scene before her now hums through its daily routine. Crumbling storefronts and faded signs that advertise hotels are wedged between modest restaurants. The makeshift sidewalks are peppered with people carrying backpacks and small shopping bags. A temporary stand has been set up to fix bicycles. Someone has hung a set of old blankets to air on a rope strung between two electric poles. Everything and everyone is coated in a film of moist, grey dust. The road that runs through is barely wide enough for the two-way honking traffic of buses, carts and motorbikes.

This place is so much more vibrant than the narrow streets of The Village of Arts and Humanities in Philadelphia, the neighborhood Lily helped to transform long before she came here. There, decay was briefly replaced by simple order if only for a few city blocks. There, the old men and young mothers watched the world from the worn-down steps of a few carefully tended red brick row houses and the painted benches of the parks they themselves had helped to create.

All that is a memory now; for Lily has not been back to The Village in a long time.

"I cannot save what I do," she says. "It was magical for me. But now it is gone; at least for me it is gone."

She wonders sometimes why she is still stuck on that feeling, why it bothers her that The Village is not the same as it was when she was there. Over a period of twenty years, the community in North Philadelphia reclaimed and converted over one hundred and fifty vacant lots into art parks, gardens, and usable space. More than ten thousand people learned new jobs and life skills in construction, renovation, art, theatre, dance, administration, computers, and cooking. Then people who lived in The Village started teaching what they learned to others in surrounding neighborhoods and schools. All this had come about because of art.

But eventually it all became much too big for her to manage. More and more of her time was spent overseeing the finances and administration. Since leaving The Village, Lily's path has taken her to other damaged communities in the world—each more different than the one before.

"I like to work in places where I can be closer to broken people," Lily says. "The broken pieces are my canvas, the stories are the ingredients, and the people are the color."

After a few minutes a short, plump woman emerges from behind the metal doors of the Dandelion Middle School. She is wearing a saggy white t-shirt splattered with green paint, black cropped pants, and brown plastic sandals with red socks. She looks at Lily through smudged round glasses and smiles. Her name is Xiao Lin. She is an art teacher here, one of Lily's apprentices.

Lily's sweet voice rises as she greets Xiao Lin and gives her a hug.

Before coming here, Xiao Lin was a factory worker in a state-owned company. Now like many of the teachers, she volunteers to help the children.

The two women step though the metal doors into a large open courtyard. The world inside the gates feels entirely different. Here children are laughing as they rush by on their way to class. In the center of the well-swept square, a group of boys and girls perform a synchronized calisthenics dance in three neat lines. The old factory building rises behind them, its expansive white façade now painted with rainbows of pink and red, green and blue. The once straight-edged roofline has been crowned in colorful triangles. Multi-hued murals and mosaics of white flowers against a periwinkle blue background decorate the walls of the surrounding buildings. Peacocks, dragons, and the phoenix fill a wall that has been constructed in front of the gatehouse. Trees have been carefully planted in rows along the edge of the space, their leaves suspended in the still heat of mid-day.

"We took inspiration for this from Chinese folk art, in particular from the paper cuttings of Ku Shu Lan. She was a famous artist from central Shaanxi province," says Lily, who came here at the invitation of the school's founder and principal in 2006. "The idea was to teach the children about part of their heritage. Ku's art is so deeply rooted. I wanted to introduce her to the students. When I started work here, I said inspiration had to come from their own culture not from outside."

The Dandelion Middle School was the first nonprofit school in the Daxing District to offer heavily subsidized, and in some cases free, education to the children of migrant workers. Local governments in China pay for education and health services for families who are formally registered in their district under something called the *Hukou* system. These social benefits do not transfer with a person if they move elsewhere in China. So when migrants come to work from villages far away, they have to find their own alternatives. The costs for schooling for non-residents are often prohibitive and the quality is poor. As a result, most parents leave their children behind. Some seventy million children across China are now growing up without their parents. The long term effects of this on the society are still unclear.

The Dandelion School was founded on the idea that a child who grows up with his or her parents has a higher probability of being a productive and well-adjusted member of society. Tuition is funded by private donors and, more recently, with income generated from the sale of small products made by teachers and students. The school enrolls a little over six hundred students between the ages of twelve to eighteen years. Challenges abound. Many students have been the victims of domestic and street violence, drugs, trauma, feelings of abandonment, and poor health. They often come with inadequate literacy skills.

When Lily arrived, she was already familiar with the long term effects of poverty and violence on families and their children. In the mid-1980s when she began her work in North Philadelphia, decades of persistent poverty had already destroyed the fiber of the community. The residents had little ability to resist the influx of drugs and crime; the neighborhood was fragmented, and the people had all but lost hope.

At first Lily did not have the context for understanding this, but in time she learned. As she toiled alone in the vacant lot cleaning up the debris and trying to figure out how to build the park she had been commissioned to create, she searched for a way to engage the people who lived there. Finally, after ignoring her repeated requests for assistance, a recovering drug addict, who had been watching her struggle for weeks, agreed to help. So did a collection of curious children who stopped to watch her work every day. At first, the unruliness of the children worried Lily, but she figured out how to redirect their energy by handing them tools and showing them how to mix cement, form sculptures, and paint. Soon she was working with the youngsters to use debris left behind in other vacant lots to build a park they helped design.

After two summers of work, *Ile Ife* Park was completed. Its name came from Nigerian cosmology and referred to the birthplace of humanity or the "House of Love." At one end was a two-story mural of a mythic owl beaming light and color to other animals below. The park itself was filled with colorful mosaic trees atop a carefully laid cobblestone fountain.

Lily's effort in the neighborhood grew even stronger when parents came to see what their children had done. They agreed to help, and in time converted other vacant lots into parks and gardens. As the physical space transformed, so too did the community and the individuals within it.

As a school bell rings, Lily stops to watch as more children pour out from one of the colorful buildings into the courtyard in front of the old factory. "We called this The Dandelion School," she says. "Because like these children, dandelions are simple, deep rooted and are everywhere. They have such strength to survive. When they blossom, they give new blossoms."

Xiao Lin beckons Lily to follow her through a covered passageway between two buildings. In a small yard beyond are two walls covered in murals. One bursts with the colorful curving branches of a tree filled with flowers. Lily calls this image, "The Tree of Life."

Scaffolding blocks a half-painted sketch on the other wall. Lined up on the ground are paint jars and buckets filled with old brushes. Xiao Lin moves them out of the way of the flow of foot traffic while Lily reaches up and takes a piece of paper that had been taped to the scaffolding. It is a sketch of the design she had in mind for the second wall. She knows, however, that others will add their own ideas and change it. Some have already painted in new images and modified what has been done. A few flowers look like pinwheels or space ships.

Knowing that this is how the process works, Lily smiles. Everyone touches a project, and you never quite know what you'll end up with. But that is the magic of it. When the wall is almost finished, Lily will pick up a brush herself and shift colors so the overall impression is more consistent. She may also touch up the background a bit to make it more interesting.

Two boys in blue and white track suits walk around her, stop and put down their packs. Lily steps back to watch as one picks up a brush, dips it in paint and holds it pointed in mid-air towards the wall. Then, without even a glance towards the two women, he leans in and begins saturating one of the flowers with yellow.

Quietly Xiao Lin climbs the scaffolding and begins work on another part of the mural. Soon others stop to watch the progress.

They laugh and say a few words. Then another boy drops his bag to join. There is no more room on the scaffolding.

When Lily first came to the Dandelion School her intent was to help transform the physical environment. She hoped that, as with North Philadelphia, this would also help change the people within it. The principal told her that almost all the children suffered from being up-rooted and, in many cases, being abandoned. Many had been left behind in their villages to fend for themselves at an early age before being reunited with their parents. Almost all lived terribly harsh lives. Beatings and abuse by family members were common. Most had behavior problems.

The first thing Lily did was to ask the students and teachers what they would like to see every day when they came to school. They told her that they wanted to be surrounded by color and elements of nature. Many had come from rural provinces and missed these places rich in natural beauty.

Lily gave paper, paints, scissors, and brushes to both the teachers and students and asked them to create whatever they wanted to express using the different media. She suggested to some that they talk to each other as they created and then to express on paper what they heard. She asked others to create something together on large sheets on the ground. The process was a release; it gave the children and their teachers permission to invent and experiment. Most importantly, it facilitated connections and communication between them that had not existed before.

One child, who had suffered both domestic violence and the imprisonment of her father, drew a picture of herself and wrote a poem that Lily still cannot forget:

It does not matter how you treat me
because I am a puppet doll
without a soul.
I don't have life so I won't die.
I don't have life so I have no pain.
I don't have life so I have no tears.
Joy, laughter — I have none because I am a puppet doll.

Lily followed with a series of workshops and projects. She asked the children to express their feelings and thoughts through drawing and poetry. The teachers then organized an exhibit and invited the children's parents. The poems that were written down revealed hurt, anger and feelings of isolation; they also expressed love for family and a longing for connection.

A fourteen year old girl wrote:

I am like a little flower; the rain has broken its tender stem.
But I believe that one day the sun will smile on me.
I am like a little bird; the wind has wrecked its wing.
But I believe that one day I will fly again.
I am a girl who has endured life's challenges.
But I believe that one day I will realize my dreams.

Another student paid tribute to her mother:

"For me you have given everything.
Through great difficulties, you nurtured me.

For me, your hair turned white, strand by strand.
Your body bent due to exhaustion.
For me you have savored bitterness
and swallowed the sour taste of life
....Mother, I know how much you have suffered and the
numerous tears you have shed for me...
I am determined to study hard."

A boy from Henan province shared what the Dandelion School had meant to him:

"Here I felt that I could root myself...
I know that I am improving myself and standing well.
I also know that my journey will not end here.
I want it to expand, expanding to the world..."

None of this surprised Lily. She had encountered similar stories in North Philadelphia and again when she worked in the slums of Korogocho, Kenya, and then in a village of survivors of the Rwandan genocide. While the brutality and suffering expressed in words and drawings was inescapable, there was almost always a ray of hope that things would someday be better.

"When you make art together you naturally talk about things you have in common like your grief," Lily says. "This is how it starts. The process is unpredictable and you must leave room in it. I've seen that when people come together to create, there is a fire that is started, and as they lay their hands on the work, it is as if that fire is nourished. You can see the transformation of the environment, but it is the transformation of minds and hearts that is the most subtle. It is a sort of alchemy."

The healing had begun at the Dandelion School and healing, according to Lily, is necessary before any rebuilding can take place. Without it, there is no solid foundation upon which to form a life or community. This had been the problem in North Philadelphia when Lily had arrived. To the outside world, the neighborhood seemed a bundle of problems against which a collection of solutions had been thrown with little result. But what everyone had neglected to see was how isolated, afraid and traumatized the people who lived there were. Working alongside the children and their parents, Lily began to see the extent of their grief. As they painted and pieced together mosaics, they spoke to each other and shared their pain and fear. The process helped them to confront what had happened and then to develop the courage and self-esteem to move forward.

"Art is an expression of yourself, and it's an empowering experience when it turns into something," Lily says. North Philadelphia was only the beginning of such empowerment. As more people heard and read about Lily, she was invited to help in places like Kenya, Rwanda, Haiti, Syria and India.

Lily does not stay at the Dandelion School full-time; she comes and goes throughout the year, returning to her home in Philadelphia and to other communities around the world where she is still working. By her third year in Shou Bao Zhuang, she felt the time was right to launch a complete transformation of the physical space. She brought with her photos of work that she had done elsewhere and shared those with the students and teachers. When the children saw these images, they grew excited about what was possible at their school. Then Lily photocopied black and white prints of the bare exterior of the old factory and surrounding buildings and asked the children to mark them up with their dream of how their school should look. Using their drawings, Lily copied elements and created sketches from which the children could begin work. After they painted murals on the old factory walls, Lily taught them about making mosaics.

Without much money, the school had to be resourceful about procuring materials. Mosaics required cement and, more importantly, colored stones, glass and ceramic to fill in the designs. Lily told the students how in North Philadelphia the community had used broken bathroom tile from demolished house sites. Was there such an opportunity here in Beijing?

There was, and the students knew exactly where to find it.

"They were so excited when they realized this and then they took us to a deserted lot where trash and tile had been dumped," Lily remembers. "We had to jump over a wall and dig to find pieces. I told them to wear gloves. Then we put the pieces in piles and transported them back to the school on bicycles and dropped it here." She motioned to the courtyard in front of the factory building. "Then we recycled it and put it on the walls."

The creative process ingrained itself in the workings of the school in many different ways. When fighting on the playgrounds became a big problem, the teachers created the "Root Cause Process" to engage the students. They took the symbol of the Tree of Life, the image that had been painted on one of the building walls, and used it as a metaphor to create a Tree of Problems. They asked the students to write what problems they saw in the school and hang them on the tree. The students filled images of dying tree fruit with words such as name calling, gang fighting, and internet games as well as other things that they believed were contributing to bad grades and bad morale. Then they discussed what the root causes of these problems were: abandonment, anger, the disappointment of their parents, and trouble in school.

The teachers then asked the students to draw a second tree and fill it with good things. This tree bore words like empathy, kindness, friends, and healthy bodies, as well as aspirations. When the drawings were complete, the teachers asked each student to sign them as a pledge to pursue the healthy tree and leave behind the Tree of Problems. They had a ceremony to honor the process and the two trees. In the months following, the principal and teachers noted that the process had an impact on behavior: disciplinary actions fell by 70%.

Xiao Lin gets down off the scaffolding and asks if Lily would like to see the work they are doing in the art studio. Lily follows her past rows of newly-planted gardens and down a long dull alleyway to the back of the school complex. The art studio is a buzz of activity. Sewing machines whir next to piles of fabric and yarn. Some of the teachers have volunteered to make small bags and are hand-stitching designs borrowed from the motifs on the walls of the school. Student- and teacher-made note cards, painted boxes, and jewelry inlaid with Lily's design work are now sold in markets in Beijing. The proceeds are helping to fund the cost of running the school a reflection of Lily's belief that it is important for students who receive assistance to give something back.

Outside again, Lily makes her way through the empty walkways and courtyards. Everyone is in class now. The bold murals remind her of all the hands that have touched them, the fire that has been created, and the lives that have changed. Lily lightly touches one of the mosaic covered walls. Pieces of her are reflected back in some of the mirror shards like a cubist painting within a painting. Her gaze falls on a mosaic bench where some of the materials have been chipped away. The children must have been climbing on it.

Lily sighs. "We cannot save all the art we create." She reaches out to touch the scar as if trying to heal it.

"The best compliment anyone gave me about my work was one day in The Village near *Meditation Park*, one of the vacant lots we had converted, I saw an older woman struggling with her walker as she moved down the street. And I wondered where she was going moving so slowly," she says. "Then she walked into the Meditation Park, sat down and looked around. I said to her, 'What can I do to help you?' She looked up at me and said, 'I just want to come and take a look.'"

Lily smiles as she remembers. It was so many years ago. "I want to create something that nobody can own in our ownership culture," she continues. "It is like a fountain. The more you take from it, the more it gives. In that moment I felt like a fountain, giving to this woman."

Lily's work at the Dandelion School is almost done. There is a low-income community in Taiwan that has invited her to come, and a refugee camp in Palestine that has also been in contact with her. She knows that what we create in the physical world is impermanent. It is the process that she wants to pass on. It is through the process that something sustainable is created.

"When I first went to North Philadelphia, I was scared as hell," she says. "But once I felt the depth of that experience, I wanted to return to it again and again. I was caught by it and in being caught, I became free." ✿

Philadelphia, U.S.A. ————————————————————

Several months after visiting the Dandelion School, I went to see Lily at home in Philadelphia. As it had been over a decade since I had been to the Village of Arts and Humanities, I asked her if we could return together to the neighborhood where her journey started.

It was a cool spring day. The cherry blossoms were in full bloom. As we walked the streets of The Village, Lily was pleasantly surprised. She had expected much more decay. But the sidewalks were swept, the roads were clean.

Small touches, like painted flower pots and mowed grass, indicated that most houses were now occupied. We passed one abandoned home, its windows and doors boarded up. Even so, someone had painted bright flowers and trees on its bleached wood surfaces.

The contrast to the adjoining areas was sobering. Only blocks away, burned out, dilapidated, and abandoned buildings fringed lots filled with refuse. Sidewalks were empty except for the occasional loitering youth. Within The Village streets it felt as if the sun always shone, while beyond it the world was dark and cold.

Only minutes after exiting Lily's car, we were surrounded by a group of burly young men in baseball caps, jeans and oversized sweatshirts. They were all smiles and deep laughs as they hugged tiny Lily. Her voice raised in excitement as she explained to me that these were some of the little troublemakers who had worked alongside her, making mosaics well over a decade ago. They had grown up, gone off to college and come back. One had just been hired to work on a project that was being launched by an organization called Mural Arts. They were going to paint murals on the sides of all the buildings down Germantown Avenue.

It had been Lily's dream to revitalize this commercial street, and now it seemed it was going to happen. Lily was excited for the young man who would be a part of this and for what she saw taking place around us. The Village was thriving. There was a growing artist colony, a small café that made fresh juices, a gathering place where musicians performed. In the parks that were converted vacant lots, children were playing, grandparents were resting, and vegetable plots were being tended. The community had built a small memorial bursting with color to those who had been killed by violence, drugs, or in service to their country.

As it was at the Dandelion School, some of the original mosaics and murals were now falling apart. The magical world of paint and tile was impermanent. But the most important transformation, that of the people who lived here, had been sustained.

I asked Lily later why she thought art had been so effective at creating lasting change. She explained that transformation happens on two levels; one has to do with the *hardware* in a community and the other with the *software*. *Hardware* is the buildings, the gardens, the homes, the parks and the services that influence the quality of lives. It is the physical world around people, the world on which outsiders focus when they evaluate the needs of a community. *Software*, on the other hand, is invisible. It is the stories, the shared values, the memories, the rituals, the traditions and trust that exist within and between people. The *software*, she says is the hardest to restore in a community after years of trauma, damage or decay. But without software the successful transformation of a person or group is unlikely.

Lily has proven that when a community such as this one uses art as a means to change its physical surroundings, it creates the space for people to come together and heal. "This is important," she says again. "Because before you rebuild, you must heal." Unfortunately, it is the step most often neglected.

What Lily has learned seems obvious now. Yet so often when we approach a problem, we are quick to design and throw money at a solution without first checking to see if the foundation is there for it to succeed. What is the emotional and spiritual state of the individuals we are trying to help? Do they have the energy or the will yet to rebuild or are they still healing?

It wasn't until midlife that Lily discovered her path. While struggling to balance her job as a professor, be a parent to a teenage son and run a household, she met Arthur Hall, who ran a dance school in North Philadelphia and was an active member of the city's art scene. He invited her to do an art project in the vacant lot next to the school building. She declined the offer. But later, in spite of warnings from friends that the neighborhood was unsafe and the residents hostile, she changed her mind.

"At first I was afraid. I wasn't afraid for my safety. I was afraid because I already had too much going on and worried I did not have enough time to do a project well. I was afraid it would consume me. I was afraid I would fail," she told me.

Lily would experience the same feeling before almost every project she undertook after this: first she would say *no*, then *yes*. In the end it was always *yes*. She admits that what worried her more than saying no was that if she didn't try, the best in her would die while the rest would amount to nothing.

Her background sheds light on this philosophy. Lily was born in China. Her father was a general in the army of Chiang Kai-shek. But there was neither a future nor security for him in China after the communists took charge. In 1948, as a young girl she fled with her family to Taiwan.

From an early age Lily studied art, in particular traditional Chinese landscape painting. In 1963, she came from Taiwan to the University of Pennsylvania to continue her studies. She has lived in Philadelphia ever since.

In spite of spending most of her life in the United States, Lily described herself several times to me as an immigrant, an outsider who was searching for a way *home*. She didn't mean *home* in the physical sense, but rather what was in her heart, her core values, what really mattered to her, who she really was. It was this quest that drew her to work in the ghetto of North Philadelphia. It is what keeps her going.

Lily's projects now span five continents and over ten countries. In addition to The Village of Arts and Humanities and the Dandelion School, she has piloted major projects in the Korogocho slum in Nairobi, Kenya; at the Mei Hua Elementary School in Daxi, Taiwan; at the Rwandan Healing Project in Rugereo Village, near Ginseyi Rwanda; and the Balata Refugee Camp near Nablu, Palestine. In 2002, she created Barefoot Artists, a nonprofit organization. She funds her work through grants and private donations.

"Perhaps because I am an immigrant woman, because I am small and invisible like a child, I have a fierce desire to be me," she says. "I feel that if any of us succumbs to the pressure or expectations that society has for us, we will lead meaningless lives."

Could she have guessed where this journey would have taken her?

"How do you know what your path in life is?" she says. "I don't think you do. You don't go out and find it. I think it is shown to you. But your heart has to be open, waiting and willing to accept it."

The man I was to meet next did exactly that.

The Healer

Give the world the best you have,
and it may never be enough;
Give the world the best you've got…anyways.

– MOTHER TERESA

Devi Shetty

The large operating theater is empty but for a cluster of men and women in green gowns hovering around a table in the middle. Next to them is a tower of machinery and monitors held together by a web of dangling tubes and cords.

Dr. Devi Shetty's white coat sets him apart from the others, as does his tall, athletic frame. A tight blue surgical cap crowns his olive complexion and dark eyes. A mask covers half his face.

"This is a four-month-old child who has a hole in the heart," he says without looking up. "If he is not operated on before he is eight or nine months, he will not get better."

A sheet hangs at one end of the table between the machinery and the patient. A tiny body is covered in blue cloth except for a small opening that reveals a cavern of human flesh. In the center of this small receptacle is a bright, red, round heart. It is the size of a walnut and glistens as the surgeon gently moves it to find the hole. His fingers isolate the point he is looking for and slowly begin to stitch.

It was Mother Teresa who noticed that Devi had a special way with children. Once during the years that he was caring for her in Calcutta she watched him tend to a small child in intensive care. She told him later that she believed God had sent him to relieve the agony of children with heart disease.

"There are many reasons I became a doctor," he says, thinking of her and the five years at the end of her life when he was asked to look after her. "But people take up special causes in their lives for different reasons. I don't think they always know why they do things initially, and then after a while it becomes something much bigger."

Working at a medical center in Calcutta, caring almost exclusively for patients who could pay for his services, the surgeon knew the traditional hospital model would have to be changed or the vast majority of his countrymen would never be able to afford healthcare. Moved by Mother's commitment to the neediest, Devi decided to become the agent of that change. He would build a hospital that would deliver first class care to the poor.

Devi left Calcutta before Mother Teresa died and returned to his home state of Karnataka in south central India. With the financial backing of his father-in-law, a successful businessman, he built Narayana Hrudayalaya, which in Sanskrit means *God's Compassionate Home*.

When it opened in 2000, one had to navigate around cows, tractors, trucks, and overcrowded buses on a dirt road leading from downtown Bangalore to the hospital. Now, financed by the bursting collection of software and outsourcing companies that flank its way, the route has been widened and paved into a viable highway.

Narayana Hrudayalaya has since been re-named Narayana Health and is more than twice the size it was ten years ago. It has over 1,000 beds, or almost five times as many as the average American hospital, and twice as many as the famed Cleveland Clinic's Heart and Vascular Institute.

Devi's surgeons perform three to seven times as many surgeries as their international counterparts, and the cost per open heart surgery is on average $2,500 versus $20,000 or more in the West. The twenty-four operating theaters can accommodate fifty surgeries a day and very often do. Over the past several years, the hospital has expanded its disciplines to include neurosurgery, gastroenterology, pediatric surgery, nephrology, urology and more.

Devi completes his work on the young child and leaves his team to finish up. Outside the operating room he takes off his surgical gloves and pulls his mask down under his chin. He believes that once in a while someone comes to earth to reassure us that God is still here, and that Mother Teresa was one such person.

"She never meant anything to be complicated. One would have thought she could have had a massive organization with millions of dollars to solve all these problems, but maybe she didn't think this was the solution for the world. She was a symbol of compassion and caring rather than someone who had a crusade to change the world," he says. "There are people like me who carry on because of her."

He makes his way up the long ramp that wraps the building like a hairpin. Unlike the quiet operating room floor, the rest of the hospital is in a state of disarray. There is, however, a sense of underlying order that keeps things from getting completely out of control. On each floor are crowds awaiting elevators, patients being moved on rolling beds and wheelchairs, clusters of families congregating outside rooms.

Devi greets and smiles at everyone. He stops at the private room of an elderly man awaiting surgery. Devi finds him comfortably resting in bed, watching television while his son helps himself to food from a small refrigerator. The doctor assures the man and his family that everything is set for the next day, then leaves.

Devi's own office is a large open room that can accommodate a gathering of fifty people and sometimes does. Through a wall of windows one sees a garden. The sound of chanting voices, a barely audible mono-melody of prayer, fills the space and separates it from the hot bustle outside.

A long brown desk commands a third of the room. Two water glasses have been neatly placed next to an untouched cup of tea. A plastic model of a heart that looks like a toy is positioned at the front of the desk.

On a matching credenza is a photograph of Devi's family. In it he is seated, wearing a blue suit and red tie. His wife, in a royal blue and gold sari, is at his side. His three sons stand solidly behind him, while his young daughter presses herself against his right arm. Next to the photograph is a view of a mountain range and script which reads: *Most of the things worth doing in the world had been declared impossible before they were done.*

In a country where the government spends only $4 a person on public health, where hospitals are overcrowded and surgeries can take months to schedule even when bribes are paid; where patients are often asked to bring their own rubber gloves, clean syringes, or lubricant gels to the hospital because there are none; finding a way to deliver healthcare to the poor does seem like an impossible task.

"The problems we have today are because we are indifferent to the issues and expect that government will solve them for us. But government can't organize a tea party in a tea garden," Devi says. He knows solving the problems of modern healthcare requires walking an unknown path, one that government is neither willing nor able to do. "In private enterprise we do not worry about the route, we worry about the destination. All the economic models that have changed industries throughout history have not affected healthcare yet because it is too fragmented. We need a radically different approach. In the U.S., they are only doing fifteen to sixteen surgeries a day. They don't think they can do more, but they can."

Patients are seated around his desk. They have been quietly waiting for him to return. Devi does not have a separate examination room. He sees everyone here in his office.

After arriving he tends to questions from his assistant, receives a quick report from a finance manager, and has a discussion with a young doctor about a diagnosis. If the patients around the desk are listening to all of this, they don't let on.

Finished with the administrative work, Devi picks up a small glass bowl full of candy and offers it to a little boy who is seated on his mother's lap at one end of the desk. Devi pulls his chair closer and sits so that he can be at eye level with the frightened child. Then he reaches out and gently touches his cheek. He speaks to the family in a mixture of Hindi and English, pulling the plastic model of the heart closer to describe the boy's condition, explain the procedure, and answer questions. His voice is soft. He tilts his head to one side as he speaks looking intently at both parents. When the mother begins to cry, Devi reassures her.

As the consultation ends, he makes notes in a file and stands up. The mother rises with him, holding her child and smiling for the first time. When Devi lifts his hand to say goodbye the boy leans away from his mother and grabs hold of it. Everyone laughs.

Devi watches them leave. He then turns to meet an old man and his son who have been sitting patiently at the other end of his desk. They have come from Assam, traveling sixty hours by train.

Next, he turns to a flat screen television and checks the angiograms of a middle-aged man from Calcutta. The files have been delivered on a laser disk. After evaluating the images, he asks the man if he is still short of breath when he walks. Not really, answers the man. Devi prescribes medicine and a change of diet and asks him to check back in four weeks' time.

"In the old days in the village there were rich people and there were poor people," Devi says. "If you were rich, you had a bigger house. But life, birth, illness and death happened equally to all. Now, you can buy life and postpone death if you have money. But if you are poor, it is not that way. You see, everyone is aspiring to make money and to improve their lives. And even if they have not yet achieved it, they still have hopes and dreams that they will. But when you tell a parent now that it will cost $1,000 to operate on their child, it is like putting a price tag on their life."

Devi's cell phone rings. Without looking to see who is calling, he hands it to his assistant who walks to a corner of the room to answer it. Meanwhile, a young woman and her parents approach the desk and quietly take their seats.

"Today people think that they are the owners of their money, but they aren't; they are just the trustees," he continues. "When God gives people the ability to create great wealth, he also gives them the responsibility for looking after society. It is very important that the fundamentals of life should be made affordable to everyone. Most of the people who come here do not have a car and may not have a house. Fair enough. Maybe they don't deserve it. But when they are in pain, when they are likely to lose someone they love because they cannot afford to have an operation, we cannot let it happen. Nowadays we are giving the right to put a price tag on human life in the hands of a few. How much longer are we going to allow this system to operate? The way things are going, if the rich remain indifferent to pain then there will be a war."

For more than an hour, people stream through Devi's office. He sees between thirty and fifty patients a day. They are young and old, Hindu, Muslim, Christian and Jain, and come from places like Orissa, Mumbai, Calcutta, Rajasthan, and even as far as Bangladesh. Some are dressed nicely, but most look as if they have come right out of the slums.

Because the quality of the work performed at Narayana Health is so good, wealthy patients come from across India and the world for complicated heart operations. Most of those on the medical team hail from some of the best schools and hospitals in the world. Here they perform about nineteen open heart surgeries a day versus about three in U.S. hospitals, according to Devi. The extent of hands-on experience is one of the attractions of working here.

"We are all paid well to live a comfortable life. I think we have been able to distinguish between need and degree. There is great spiritual reward in saving so many lives that might otherwise have been lost," says Devi.

One of the reasons Narayana Health works is because of the approach taken to build it. Traditional healthcare systems are created from the bottom up. At the base is the primary care network of general practitioners. Above this is secondary care, provided by specialists that a patient accesses through referrals. Finally, tertiary care is added to the mix; surgeons like Devi who serve admitted patients.

Devi does not believe, however, that this traditional model is effective or financially viable in the long term. "In primary healthcare there is no money to support the cost structure," he explains. "But when large organizations like ours take on a specialty in tertiary care, excel at it and make money, then with the proceeds we are able to offer primary and secondary healthcare affordably to many more people." The profit margins on tertiary care are much higher than for primary care.

One-third of the operations performed at Narayana Health are on patients who can afford to pay for the procedures. Some incur additional fees for private rooms and amenities. Another one-third of the patients afford treatment thanks to a micro-health insurance plan devised by Devi and run by the government. The final one-third consists of patients who cannot afford care or insurance and are in a life-threatening condition. They pay what they can while the remaining expense is covered by the hospital's own charitable arm and the profits that the hospital makes from other patients. Most of these patients are children who have no other hope for survival. Narayana Health does more pediatric heart surgeries now than any other hospital in the world. The children treated come from more than seventy different countries, many of those in the developing world.

A year after Devi started Narayana Health, he launched a telemedicine network, in partnership with the Indian Space Research Organization, which provided connectivity to reach millions who live in rural India with no access to cardiac care. There are over fifty-four telemedicine centers in India where patients come with their doctors to seek professional consultation. Via video conferencing they speak with doctors at Devi's hospital. Angiograms and other test images are transported over high-speed satellite technology from the local centers to Narayana Health.

Telemedicine helped to cure over 18,000 patients within the first four years of operation. Today there are over five hundred telemedicine centers around the world, all networked back to expert doctors in Bangalore and Calcutta, where Devi has created another center.

In a small conference room near his office, a flat television screen, a computer monitor, a chair, a camera on a tripod, and some high-level lighting, have been set up. Devi takes a seat in the chair and looks into the camera. On the screen in front of him are three figures sitting in a sparse room somewhere far away. Because of the video conferencing technology they are able to look straight at Devi. The patient, Mr. Chatterjee, is an older man. Beside him is a younger man wearing a physician's coat. Behind them is another young man, the patient's son.

When Devi turns to the computer, a technician projects a black and white image of a heart inside a bony chest cavity. The two rooms are silent while Devi examines the images. After a few minutes Devi asks the physician on the monitor what the recommendations were from the doctors in their location. There is more discussion and then Devi addresses the patient directly. "Are you able to go for a walk?" The old man nods and grunts.

"When was your heart attack?"

"The 18th of January," the old man replies.

"Mr. Chatterjee, I would like you to wait three months. In that time your heart will improve greatly. After three months, I would like you to come to Bangalore, and we will take a look. You continue with all your medicines now and I will see you then. Are there any other questions, Mr. Chatterjee?"

Mr. Chatterjee's son asks about dietary restrictions. Devi gives him some guidelines. When the consultation is done, the three men stand. Mr. Chatterjee puts his two hands together and bows. "Thank you sir," he says.

After four more consultations, the camera is switched off. Devi gets up from his chair. He is ready for the next meeting.

"It is a really fascinating world," he says. "My teachers treated patients whom they could touch. Today we can treat patients in Calcutta, Africa, and Malaysia, anywhere that we have a center. That completely changes the dynamics of care. Healthcare is nothing but knowledge, so when you ask the right question you start the process of getting the right care. It is not rocket science. Here you see the most extreme end of the spectrum: operating on the heart. But the bulk of healthcare is not complicated, and basic healthcare can be given by almost anyone."

Technology has helped his team to do better work, including learning in real-time from experts in other parts of the world. Children's Hospital in Philadelphia has the largest experience base in the world in transplants for kids. "We've been able to tie up with them and link our operating rooms," Devi says. "Their anesthesiologist can see the operating screen and are telling ours what to do. We are receiving real time feedback from them."

Heart disease is a leading killer in India. The average age for a heart attack victim is forty-five versus sixty-five in the rest of the world. Devi thinks the reasons are primarily genetic, although there are growing environmental risks, too.

The disease makes no distinction between rich and poor. Anyone can be a victim.

So in addition to telemedicine centers, Devi's team created mobile diagnostic labs: buses, staffed by cardiologists and technicians. These mobile teams travel at least five hundred miles from Bangalore and Calcutta to screen the very poor in rural areas and those who cannot afford the cost or the time to travel long distances to hospitals. These mobile units can screen four hundred people a day for their vital statistics and cholesterol levels.

The screenings are free for patients, paid for by the Narayana Hrudayalaya Charitable Trust. They are not a cure, but do open the door to early warning and prevention. They also provide an informal feedback loop to Narayana Health about what is working and what needs to be modified. There is still the challenge, however, of providing affordable options for the people who actually have serious, life threatening conditions.

The charitable arm of the hospital cannot afford to support the millions of poor patients who fall into this category. So the Narayana Health team designed a micro-insurance plan for providing health insurance for poor farmers. In a country where healthcare costs were the primary source of indebtedness among the poor, this was a revolutionary idea.

For the equivalent of about $2 a year, a farmer can join the Yeshasvini Health Insurance Scheme. Though conceived by Devi Shetty and his colleagues, the program is administered separately by the state government and an independent healthcare organization based in Delhi. The insurance provides patients with access to one hundred and fifty hospitals in twenty-nine districts for treatment costing up to the equivalent of $2,000. In its first year, 9,000 people underwent surgeries and 35,000 people received outpatient treatments. Now over ten million people belong to the program.

It is time for lunch and Devi moves to a meeting room next to his office. He has brought a collection of metal tins from home filled with cooked food. A man and woman are waiting for him behind piles of papers. They are not eating. Where their lunch boxes might have been are spreadsheets and calculators.

The trio first reviews the inventory of hospital supplies: clips, artery stents, oxygen and surgical gloves. The man gives a full account of the size of the orders and the costs. He notes how it has changed over the past five years and by how much costs have risen and continue to increase.

"When we order one hundred coronary artery stents, how do we know we get one hundred?" asks Devi.

"There is a person who opens the boxes when they arrive and counts them," says the woman.

"How do they know that this is exactly what we ordered in terms of quality and price? Who are these people who are checking the material?" asks Devi.

"These are the same people who have always done this job in the receiving area," the man says.

"I would like to see our costs and number per day including labor hours, maintenance and outsourcing costs," says Devi.

"We can do a weekly average," offers the man.

"I'd like a daily analysis."

The man and women initially look panicked, but then nod their heads, collect their papers, and leave the room.

"Even though we are over $60 million in revenues, I oversee every check that is written," says Devi. "As we get bigger things can become more expensive if we do not pay attention. I remind everyone that our supplies are not being paid for by management, but by a poor lady with a baby in her hands. Every day hundreds of mothers come to us. They sell everything they have and give the money to us to save their child's life. We have a great responsibility and are the trustees of that money. We will use every penny of it to help the child, not waste it."

Narayana Health is big enough now to have the buying power to negotiate volume discounts on supplies and medicine. Many of the medical equipment manufacturers offer state of the art imaging and diagnostic equipment to them in return for Narayana's agreement to test it. Because the volume of cases is so high at Narayana Health, an equipment manufacturer can get quicker feedback on their products than from other hospitals. Devi knows he is one of the biggest buyers in India and has used this to their benefit.

In addition to materials and equipment, Narayana Health manages its compensation differently than other hospitals. Salaries of doctors and staff make up 22% of total costs versus 60% in the United States. One reason for this is that a hospital in India does not need to employ as many people to process the multitude of private insurance, Medicare, and Medicaid paperwork. But this does not account for the entire gap. The main factor is that doctors are paid much less at Narayana Health relative to the revenues that they bring in. Each surgeon receives a fixed salary regardless of the number of surgeries he or she does, not a percentage of revenues, as is the practice in many other places.

"If you want to last, you need to make yourself financially viable, no matter who you are," Devi explains. "Today nobody has enough money to sustain you just because they like your cause. Philanthropy is not the solution for the world, because philanthropy depends on someone being able to give, in order for you to keep doing what you do." Devi believes that by using the resources they have to their fullest potential, they can deliver low cost healthcare, while improving the quality of what they do as they gain more experience.

When it is well past dinner time, Devi still has a line of patients outside his door. He will be working into the night. Despite all the projects he is launching and the day-to-day operations he oversees, he leaves enough time every day for the people who need him most.

"The moment you stop seeing your patients you are lost," he says. "In healthcare, you must always be a doctor first no matter what the other demands. If you cease to be a doctor, after a while you will stop innovating and finding ways to save lives." ❁

Bangalore, India _____

After hearing about Devi Shetty from a friend in Bangalore, I decided to include him in one of our forums because, like our participants, he was a leader of a large organization, tackling challenges with limited resources. The first time I reached out to him I called his cell phone and his assistant answered. After I explained who I was and named the person who had referred me, the phone was given to Devi, who said he'd be happy to see me.

I was surprised that a busy heart surgeon who also ran a large hospital would be willing to meet a complete stranger. Perhaps he thought I would bring influential visitors with deep pockets. Maybe he was just open to the unexpected.

I formed an image for myself of Devi before our first meeting. I imagined an energetic, focused, efficient and occasionally impatient man. I expected him to be like other leaders I knew who successfully ran large organizations: pleasant, polite, straight to the point, with no time to waste on idle chat. He was all these, except he was patient, and that is what I liked most about him. There was something about his calm and gentle disposition that drew people in and kept them close and committed to his mission.

The woman who runs his charitable wing spoke for many when she said, "My God, he is an inspiration. But for him, I would not have done this much. He says *God bless you and God will help you if you help others.* This principle is policy. He is a great man with a great vision. And it is our duty to make his dream come true." She works directly with Devi on many things, and he has told her that he will support whatever decisions she makes on the job. It is that kind of confidence in people that make this a good place to work, she said.

She also noted that none of the doctors are there for the money. "If your eyes are on the money then your focus is elsewhere, not on the poor and their suffering. That is happening in other places. Here you sacrifice a lot to help. It is not possible to help everyone in the world, but I know I do one or two good deeds a day by the time I go home."

When I asked Devi how he and his team came up with new ideas, he said there were about fifty men and women who were always talking and working on things. Included in that group was his son Viren, who managed the supply chain, as well as his wife who paid the bills.

"Mobile phones are the greatest gift to us," Devi said. "When we are stuck in traffic for half an hour, we can talk to each other. Most of the time what we come up with doesn't work, but one or two ideas do. Never be scared to make mistakes. Do lots of things. Some work out, some don't. When it doesn't, you have learned something."

Devi was educated in India and did his cardiac training at West Midlands Cardiothoracic Rotation Program in England followed by an appointment at Guy's Hospital London in the Cardiothoracic Unit. In the late 1980s, he returned to India to be the Chief Cardiac Surgeon at the BM Birla Heart Research Center in Caluctta. He was only thirty-three years old. During these years he met and cared for Mother Teresa. A decade later he returned to Bangalore and founded Narayana Hrudayalaya.

"I come from a business family. If I had grown up in India in a different time, maybe I would have been one of those freedom fighters or a teacher. It was fascinating to learn medicine though," he said.

While Lily Yeh had found a way to make her effort self-sustaining by having the people with whom she worked be the solution, Devi had found a different way to sustainability. Perhaps it is because of his business heritage that he has been able to draw lessons from that discipline to run his hospital. Like any good business person, he first made sure he understood the needs of his "customers" and the different ways he might serve those needs. For most people there was no viable or affordable option for healthcare in India. For the few who could afford medical care, there were limited first choices. In that was the opportunity.

Convinced that people would pay for quality, Devi built a team of talented doctors and created the conditions under which they could become even better in order to serve their "customers." He was right, and with those profits, Narayana Health could finance care for those who couldn't pay.

Healthy profits are a result not only of increasing revenues, but of tight cost controls. Devi's team ruthlessly managed the bottom line — always mindful that costs were being paid for by that poor woman with a sick baby in her hands. Profits were maximized to further fund the mission of delivering healthcare to the poor.

Finally, Devi and his team never lost perspective on the reality that they cannot take anything of material value with them when they die. This underlies one of their core values: we are only the custodians of the things we acquire and the money we make. Those who have achieved so much, have the responsibility to care for others who have so little.

Today Devi continues to formalize the management of Narayana Health and has drawn from some of India's top technology companies to supplement his team with expertise in human resources, marketing and information management. He has also launched a low-cost hospital in Mysore, where heart operations can be completed for as little as $800. There the focus has been on using pre-fabricated materials in construction, measured use of utilities, and diligent supply chain management to keep expenses down.

During one of my visits to Narayana Health, I asked Devi if he thought that in the world today, particularly the developed world, it is possible that we have abdicated our personal responsibility for caring for one another to large organizations and governments.

"Yes we have, while knowing all along that they are inefficient at what they do," he replied. "But what is the alternative? Individual initiatives like ours? There is no precedence in the world for what we are doing. If we are able to create an alternative model that works, then we will have the right to move forward this way. Social transformation does not happen on ideas or theoretical models."

Devi asked that any story I told focus on his hospital and what his team had done together, not on him. He didn't want the personal attention. I assured him that I was more interested in the story of an ordinary person who realized he could make a difference by committing to use his talents in the service of others. Perhaps that story would inspire others to believe that they, too, could do something similar with their lives, I said. He was happy with that.

A few days after my visit to Narayana Health, I travelled to the slums of Mumbai to meet with another ordinary man. Early in his life, he too had recognized that large organizations and governments are inefficient and ineffective at solving problems. As a result, he committed himself to bringing about social transformation through the most practical of means and demonstrating to governments all over the world how to affect meaningful change.

The Organizer

The real test of a man is not how well
he plays the role he has invented for himself,
but how well he plays the role
that destiny assigned to him.

– VACLAV HAVEL

Jockin Arputham

The first thing one notices about Jockin Arputham is his eyes. When he is amused they are alight; when he is angry they are as stones; when he has heard it all before, they roam above the heads of those talking as if searching for alternatives. It is only when confronted with injustice that they become dark and still.

Jockin stands tall at five feet. His small, curious face is adorned with round wire glasses giving him the look of an owl. His head is crowned by thinning grey hair, his chin shadowed by razor stubble. He wears the common man's uniform of Mumbai: a white-collared shirt, un-tucked and hung over grey pants with a crease carefully pressed down the front. For most of his life, Jockin has been barefoot—though occasionally he slips into a filthy pair of rubber flip flops when he heads out into the streets, a habit he grudgingly adopted when he started to travel outside his slum to meet with people in other places in the world. Jockin is in his late seventies.

Yet the old slum *walla* (a term used to describe someone who hails from the slums) has the energy of someone half his age.

The sun is beating on his bare head, launching rivulets of perspiration down his neck as he makes his way across the busy intersection on the edge of Dharavi, Asia's largest slum. The dust churned up by the herd of passing trucks, cars, and motorcycles fills his nose. There are no sidewalks here, just a rough no-man's-land between the huts on the side of the road and the traffic snarl that makes its way across the city of Mumbai.

He passes several crooked buildings that house cramped shops with large openings like garage doors. Stacks of timber overflow into the street in front of a business that re-sells old building materials collected from all over the city. The next doorway is filled with piles of neatly arranged rectangular tins reflecting the dirty sunlight. They have been collected from trash bins and garbage piles. Once cleaned and restored they will be sold to vendors who will fill them with oil and re-sell them. In another shop, young men stuff soft plastics and drink bottles into large bags. There are over one thousand recycling businesses like these in Dharavi.

More than half of Mumbai's population live in slum settlements. Dharavi is the largest with over 800,000 residents. At one time it was a dump site full of water on the outskirts of the city. Later it was set aside for the hordes of poor migrants who came from rural India to find work. But as Mumbai grew and stretched northward, Dharavi found itself planted in the middle of a bustling metropolis and next to the shiny and new business district of Worli. Its relative geography has now made it coveted land for developers who seek to capitalize on the city's booming economy.

Dharavi is a cultural and economic mosaic. Muslims from Tamil Nadu have built the leather tanning industry. Embroiderers from Uttar Pradesh run a vibrant garment business. Others from the south have brought sweet-making techniques which have grown into a flourishing prepared food industry. Three-quarters of the residents run small businesses here, while the remainder works as taxi drivers, office workers or maids in other parts of the city. Monthly incomes for residents range from $10 to $1,000. These are the backs upon which the Indian miracle has been built.

Jockin says that in spite of what you think you see before you, a slum is nothing more than a human habitation. A slum is only a slum because the buildings are built by the people who live there, not by someone else, and because it is missing many necessary and basic services such as waste removal, running water, and toilets that are available in more affluent parts of the city. Most of the structures are built of permanent materials like cement or brick and have two stories. Many of those are rented at rates ranging from $10-$40 a month depending on the location and conditions of the slum. About a quarter of these structures is made from temporary materials and is vulnerable to demolition and land clearing.

"There is no slum-free city in the world now," Jockin says. "And Mumbai will never be slum-free. There is already a backlog in housing demand here. We need to envision a future of slum-friendly cities because a slum is nothing more than a dwelling place. It is a vibrant location and community where people know who is coming or going. It is not a middle-class society, but it is a positive place where people live next to each other, share, and have concern for each other. If a person is having a hard time and cannot find food to eat, people in the slum will look after them."

While in countries like the United States less than 6% of the urban population lives in slums, more than half the residents of cities in the developing world do. The percentage is increasing each year, as more people migrate from rural areas across Asia, Africa, and Latin America in search of opportunity in these growing urban centers.

Jockin steps off the main road through a dark doorway leading to a narrow set of stairs that takes a steep turn between two dilapidated buildings. A young woman in a bright orange sari stands in an open doorway holding her baby. She greets Jockin as he walks by. Others nearby do the same. Everyone knows him. He has been the unofficial leader of the slum dwellers of India for over forty years.

Eventually the cave-like descent opens into sunshine and the slum walla pauses atop a long sewer pipe. On either side of the orb, far below, are piles of dirty plastic, wet cloth, string, rubber and human waste. A trickle of toxic purple water winds through the thick sludge.

For decades the residents of this and other slums in the city paid a monthly rent to the municipality for each of their allotted plots of land. They received little in return. The city did not provide a clean water supply, sewage system, toilets, or garbage collection and disposal.

This reality motivated Jockin at a young age to organize a group of children and their parents to march on city hall and leave behind bags of trash. To avoid bad publicity, the government had grudgingly agreed to improve some of the conditions in which they lived, but nothing significant. The experience inspired Jockin to begin mobilizing people around other issues, and in time he became the community organizer that he is today.

Three small children rush past, almost knocking him into the cesspool below. He balances atop the pipe like a tightrope walker until he finds a spot to step off and onto a soft, wet path. He walks through a narrow lane that twists haphazardly, a result of spontaneous construction, not city planning. If he wanted to, he could reach out with both arms and touch the buildings on either side. Above him the light of the hot sky is obstructed by mezzanine overhangs. Underfoot are layers of gooey mud. All around is the smell of human sweat, oil and excrement.

Because Dharavi was originally unplanned there was no sewage system in place to carry away waste. To compensate for this, the government built self-contained toilet blocks in many of the neighborhoods; but the effort was short-lived. As a result there are too few toilets, and they are rarely, if ever, maintained. When the slum dwellers, under Jockin's leadership, did a survey of 151 slums in Mumbai, they discovered that there was one toilet seat for approximately every 1,500 persons and that 80% of those toilets didn't work. The lines to use those that do work are long, and the lack of privacy a deterrent for women who fear for their safety, particularly at night.

The muddy lane opens onto a main street where a collage of brightly colored Hindu women mix with simple-covered Muslims going about their daily chores. Old men squat on sidewalks, shaded from the hot sun, sleepily observing the passing world. A young man shouts a greeting at Jockin from a sundries stall. The slum walla nods. A small truck takes up most of the street and obstructs the way for other vehicles trying to get by. The sound of honking horns is deafening. Jockin shoos away a stray goat that blocks his way.

Down a nearby side street is a new toilet block that the slum dwellers have built themselves. It took years to get support to do this. But finally, the municipal government agreed to pay the capital costs of constructing community designed toilet blocks, if the communities agreed to their ongoing management and maintenance. This particular toilet has separate rooms for men, women and children. The neighbors keep it clean.

The slum dwellers have constructed more than 800 toilet facilities and are still building. By taking on this responsibility, they have also solved the problem of access to basic water service. By order of the municipality, water must be piped in when a new toilet block is built. If existing structures are in the way, water holding tanks are installed. The water intended for toilets can now also be tapped into for daily household needs.

These days, however, it isn't toilets that the community leaders are talking about. They are focused on a much more pressing issue: the redevelopment of Dharavi. The government has announced plans to divide the slum into five sectors and auction each off to a different commercial developer. Under the terms of the sale, developers must provide alternative housing for the current residents.

This seems like a simple solution to wash the scourge of a slum away and replace it with more attractive real estate. But Jockin knows that if the poor do not have a voice in this process, the developers will build housing that suits their objectives, not those of the slum dwellers. Profit might be maximized by constructing twenty-story high rises on small parcels of land where one family lives on top of another. But this approach would wipe out the thriving neighborhoods that exist today as well as the markets and small businesses that provide the livelihood for three-quarters of the residents. The social and economic impact could be devastating, the long term effect on the city disastrous.

"It's very dangerous to arbitrarily clear out a slum. When you do, you remove the quality of co-dependence, and then you create another problem," says Jockin. "Outsiders think a slum is a place of crime and that the people there are lazy. They think people are fooling around and not doing hard work, that they are pickpockets. But these are notions of people who are not involved here or who have never been here."

Later this morning Jockin will attend a meeting with some of the developers who plan to bid on the Dharavi land. He knows they see a way to make ten times their investment if they prevail, so the discussion will be heated. "This land belongs to the people who settled here, to whom the government gave it when no one else wanted it," he says. "These citizens have rights, too." It has been Jockin's life mission to ensure the poor know their rights in India's democracy and are empowered to exercise them.

The impending re-development of Dharavi is only the latest of the battles he has taken on. The first was in the 1970s in Janata Colony, the slum where Jockin lived when he came to Mumbai as a teenage runaway. Upon learning that his slum was to be razed and the residents evicted, Jockin organized demonstrations by his fellow slum dwellers. At one point 50,000 came together to protest against the planned evictions.

Jockin learned that, as citizens, the slum dwellers had a right to make their case in court. For months he and a small group poured over city records and met with retired officials to gain evidence to prove that Janata Colony was a legitimate settlement and thus should not be arbitrarily razed. At one point Jockin travelled to Delhi to get a face-to-face meeting with Prime Minister Indira Gandhi. But she would not see him.

As a poor young man, Jockin had very little leverage in the formal system. But his intelligence and charisma won over the masses. When the distribution of handbills was declared illegal, Jockin and his team resorted to hiding them rolled up in *chapattis* (a flat loaf of bread), or wetting them and sticking them to the top of ambulances so they would blow off and be picked up by people all over the city.

His tactics made everyone take notice. He led demonstrations and even once threatened to blow up a building if the demolitions took place.

The movement gained momentum as common ground was forged between more neighborhood and community leaders. In 1974 Jockin formalized these relationships into the National Slum Dwellers Federation (NSDF). Today NSDF spans cities across India and effectively negotiates and works with governments on behalf of the urban poor.

Despite the good fight for Janata Colony, nothing could stop the demolition. In May 1976, the massive destruction began. It took forty-five days to complete. Jockin's work was not in vain, however. His organizers managed to ensure that everyone who had lived there was given a new site in a slum on the east side of the city that had been provisioned with toilets, schools, police stations, water pipes and health centers.

Now he has a similar fight on his hands in Dharavi. This time the stakes are much greater. Instead of 50,000 citizens being affected, the number is closer to one million.

Jockin turns off the busy road into a vacant lot surrounded by rundown, low-lying buildings housing small apartments. A group of local community leaders is waiting for him. He makes his way to the entrance of one of the buildings while the men fall in step behind him. A collection of dirty rubber sandals is scattered in front of the open door. He slips his off and steps inside.

On the far wall of the room is a large map with an aerial view of the slum. Beneath it, gathered on the floor, are women pouring over sheets of paper. They glance at Jockin when he enters, then return to their work. They are compiling the data they have collected about who lives in each hut on each street. There are no official enumerations, maps, or surveys for slums in Mumbai, so the women are gathering census information that will not only help to build a case for basic services in their communities, but also provide valuable data for the government to use in its planning process.

There was a time when the government wouldn't even grant an audience with the poor, but today the bureaucrats and the slum dwellers often work together. "It is easy enough to criticize the government," says Jockin, "but if you want things to change, you have to establish a relationship with them."

In 1985, after years of fighting the government, Jockin began to explore different strategies for moving the urban poor agenda forward in India. At first he partnered with various non-government organizations. It did not take long to discover that this approach would not work. The NGOs preferred to use a relationship with Jockin to build a case for getting more funds, rather than listening first to what he needed.

"At that time, NGOs from all over wanted to help poor Indians," he says. "They all came and found me. But in time I realized that we were altogether different in our thinking. For example, I was fighting for drinking water in the slums, and they wanted to plant trees so we would have green space. I said to them, 'We don't even have drinking water, so how are we going to plant and care for trees?'"

Jockin also tried working with the trade unions which had established influence with the government. Soon, however, he realized they were just interested in representing the formal working class and not the informal working class or the very poor. "An urban poor movement has to include *all* of the poor," he says.

About this time, Jockin encountered SPARC, an NGO working with women who lived on the pavement. He quickly realized that this NGO was different than others; SPARC did not profess to have answers, nor did it have programs that had worked elsewhere that could be applied here. Instead, it was willing to let the poor set the agenda for what had to be done and then support them in their efforts.

SPARC had been founded by a woman named Sheela Patel and a group of her middle class colleagues who had broken away from a government-supported social service to establish their own effort. They worked with the women and families who lived on the street. Known as footpath wallas, or pavement dwellers, they were the poorest of the poor, living in shacks erected with whatever materials could be scavenged or procured. There on the pavement, the footpath wallas raised their children, cared for their elders, worshiped their gods, and mourned their dead.

In the late 1980s, the pavement dwellers had, with encouragement from SPARC, formalized their effort. They now call themselves *Mahila Milan* (Women Together) and have become an integral part of Jockin's coalition that includes SPARC and NSDF.

Jockin knows it is difficult for outsiders to understand the many levels of poverty here. Some slum dwellers do very well for themselves and even own their shacks. They have television sets and other amenities. Most of them are formally employed in small businesses or working for someone else. At the opposite end of the spectrum are the pavement dwellers who work in informal jobs—selling small items on the streets, as domestic help, as street cleaners, or as prostitutes. They live together in *zopadpattis*, or hutments, side by side along busy streets, railway lines, and airport runways—anywhere they can find open space. They have no claim to the land they are on; they are squatters, and their situations are tenuous at best.

For years the pavement dwellers struggled alone. Even though they knew their neighbors, they barely had enough to survive themselves, let alone help one another. But in 1986, shortly after they began working with SPARC, something happened that not only changed the pavement dwellers' lives and the conditions under which they lived, but also helped to fuel a new movement of the urban poor world-wide.

Jockin was in the SPARC office in Byculla in south central Mumbai when a group of women from a local *zopadpatti* came rushing in. Someone had posted a demolition notice on one of their shacks, they said. Demolitions of hutments were common in Mumbai. Whenever the pavement dwellers heard rumors of impending destruction, they panicked. The men ran to their local elected councilors to try to get the demolition stopped; the women prepared themselves and their family for the aftermath.

Everyone had an assignment. Most of the women worked domestic help jobs nearby so that when a demolition came they could get home quickly. The young children were trained as runners who spread the word that the trucks were coming. The older children were responsible for collecting the families' belongings.

The routine became sickeningly familiar. The demolition teams wiped out everything and then carted it all away. It took weeks, if not months, to rebuild what had been lost. The process kept the pavement dwellers perpetually impoverished with little hope of things ever improving.

Desperate to break this cycle, on this day the women went to find Jockin to tell him what had happened. The slum walla listened and then called a meeting of the residents of this particular hutment. He asked everyone to tell what they knew. They explained how someone came and posted the notice, how the demolition was scheduled for some time soon, how the men in the settlement went to the government to talk about it, what the elected official said to them, and so on. They didn't know what day or time the demolition would be; it could be a week or two weeks away.

As the stories were recounted, the residents had an epiphany. They stopped seeing themselves as individual families struggling to survive, but instead as a group bound together by a common challenge. Jockin then organized them into teams and sent them out to learn more. Soon, they reported to the community that there was a demolition squad, an engineering squad, and an individual in charge of the effort. They re-constructed how the local ward office was organized and operated. They were building a shared understanding of how things worked through the collective experience of storytelling. It was clear that the politicians they had elected were not acting in their interest. They learned that if no notice had been posted in advance of a demolition, they had the right to stop it. They started taking photographs of the trucks and men who carted away their possessions so they could track down and reclaim what was theirs under the law. In time, however, they learned that if they really wanted things to change, they needed to have a dialogue with the government representatives ultimately responsible for these demolitions. These were not the elected representatives but rather the Municipal Commissioner (the appointed chief executive of the city) and the non-elected bureaucracy beneath him.

Aware that they lacked the tools and connections to initiate this dialogue, the pavement dwellers looked for help. With the support of the middle class women in SPARC, they launched a letter-writing campaign to the Municipality. As the pavement dwellers were illiterate, the women from SPARC wrote on their behalf. The letters introduced the settlement, the number of houses and the families who lived there. The women explained they had been saving to find better housing because they didn't want to live on the street. They asked for more time before demolition and requested a meeting in hopes of finding an alternate solution.

Letter writing became a group effort, and each letter was signed either by *Mahila Milan*, SPARC, or National Slum Dwellers Federation. The three-pronged strategy started to work. Bureaucrats began paying attention. The pavement dwellers were granted an audience with the municipal government.

When they arrived for the meeting, the pavement dwellers were surprised to learn that security had been called in case things got out of hand. But in time, as everyone got to know one another, the meetings progressed smoothly. The women learned that there were reasons for the demolitions. In one case, for example, the government wanted to clear the pavement of the hutments because they were planning a road-widening project.

Jockin insisted that every time the women learned something new they should meet and share. He knew there was no shortcut to discovery; this was a process that took a long time. In an effort to build solidarity between hutments, he invited leaders from other pavement settlements in the city to share what they were experiencing. In this way the movement began to grow and gain momentum. For the first time, the poorest of the poor felt their power. Jockin was on a mission to unite all classes of the urban poor. He felt that once empowered with knowledge of their legitimate rights, the citizens could speak with one voice and affect greater change in India's urban centers.

Eventually, the government realized a relationship with the movement could be mutually beneficial. When the State Collectors office needed a survey of how many people were living in an informal settlement that flanked the railway lines in Mumbai, it asked for help from SPARC, which had become the "legitimate" interface between the urban poor and the government bureaucracy. When the government granted money for enumerations work that they knew would be done by slum and pavement dwellers, it wrote the checks to SPARC with the understanding that the NGO would oversee the work and manage the money. In reality it was Jockin and the community leaders who organized and oversaw the work.

But both SPARC and Jockin knew that the government would be more comfortable giving money to a legitimate organization than a group of slum dwellers. So they set it up such that SPARC took the money and then channeled it to the poor who did the work.

As it grew, *Mahila Milan* created a savings collective. Each day, each woman contributed a small amount to a joint account managed by the group. From these collected funds, loans were given to start small businesses or for personal emergencies. These loans were almost always paid back.

Jockin also encouraged the women to start saving money in order to someday buy homes of their own. Then he sent them out to find suitable land. On weekends they took picnics to the city limits to inspect potential sites. They prioritized the land that they saw and began building a case to present to the government.

Once this process had begun, Jockin tasked the women with designing a model house that would meet their needs and be affordable. Using the lengths of their saris as a measuring tool they created three prototypes and filled them with beds and utensils. Then they invited other pavement dwellers as well as members of the government and bureaucracy to come and see.

The government members were stunned. They had underestimated these women.

The prototypes remained on display at the SPARC offices for a week. Jockin invited a mason, who was also a slum dweller, to help the women estimate how many bricks would be required to build each prototype and how much each brick would cost. Through this process, the pavement dwellers learned the importance of asking good questions.

In the months following, the women of *Mahila Milan* along with a couple of women from SPARC travelled by train across India to visit low cost housing communities. These settlements had been constructed by various local governments and NGOs without the input of the poor. The women saw that most of these structures had been made of materials that were not only impractical, but also costly to maintain. They were also located on land far away from their workplaces, making it difficult for them to support themselves. In some cases, the pavement dwellers had sold the houses they had been given and returned to the streets so they could be close to their jobs. Learning how other cities had handled resettlement reinforced the importance of demanding a voice in the process.

When they were ready, the women of *Mahila Milan* began designing their own homes in earnest. They wanted to make them small, but airy and clean. To save space they would build common toilets to be shared by six or ten families with separate rooms for women, men, and children. Private toilets would be a waste of valuable space as one only used that spot in the house a few times a day anyway.

At last the women were ready and they had the government on their side. The big question was land and where to find it, because in Mumbai no matter what class you are a part of, everyone is competing for the same land. As Jockin knows all too well, it is those with the power who usually win that battle. But he also knows now that power comes in different forms. It takes both persistence and knowledge to realize your power, and they have both.

Jockin has one day in Dharavi between trips to deal with the issues that have arisen during his absence. Tomorrow, he leaves for Brazil where he will visit community leaders in the slums of Sao Paolo. They are a part of Slum Dwellers International (SDI), a worldwide federation of urban poor that Jockin helped to found in 1996.

Today SDI involves community leaders from one hundred and fifty cities across Asia, Africa and Latin America. The model is similar to what Jockin started in India: the poor set the agenda and the NGOs they ally with help them to get the resources and make the necessary connections to get things done. Fundamental to the federation's work is the sharing of learning between members in their quest to secure housing and rights in their respective cities. What works? they ask each other. What doesn't?

Although Jockin spends a good amount of his time on SDI business, he has not forgotten the people of Mumbai. There is a stream of people lining up outside the door now, waiting to meet with him. They are seeking his counsel on questions and issues having to do with housing, water, toilets, police, or trash. Though great gains have been made, there are still many problems to tackle.

Jockin places his cell phones side by side on the low table in front of his chair. He carries two now because one is not enough to manage the volume of calls he gets. One phone rings and he picks it up to talk. "..Yes sir....oh...ya...ya...ya." No sooner has he finished, then the other starts to ring. He picks that one up, and the first one rings. This goes on for a few minutes until he turns both phones over and hits the "end" button. Then he turns his attention to the people sitting at his feet.

After a couple of hours the line outside is no shorter, but it is time for the Dharavi re-development meeting, and he must go. Jockin knows that there has to be a plan for the future of Dharavi. Who determines that plan will have far reaching effects for the city of Mumbai and everyone who lives here. The poor are entirely capable of playing a meaningful role in this process—they have proved it time and again-- and they must be allowed to do so.

"Dharavi has to change," he says. "People need better facilities, better amenities and more space. But the architect of this particular redevelopment plan sees the solution as top down, a public-private partnership to clean up the place. When you do not consult the people who live here, then development is not sustainable. It took the UN forty years to realize this. Finally Kofi Annan made it very clear that development must happen from the bottom up."

Jockin gets up and makes his way to the door. As he searches among the pile of sandals for his own, a group of children who have been playing on the nearby dumpsters run up and encircle him. He wraps his hands around their soft, dark heads. Curling their ears he scolds them gently for blocking the way. He laughs, and they laugh.

"If you want to mobilize a community you have to start with understanding what people want for their children," he says. "If you ask them you won't have to guess. From that you will know what to do." ✾

Mumbai, India ───────────────────────────────

On one of my many trips to Mumbai, I spent an afternoon with the women of *Mahila Milan* and Celine D'Cruz, one of the co-founders of SPARC. Celine was raised in a middle class family in Mumbai but by the time I met her she had spent more than half her life working in the slums. While in university, she was employed with a welfare agency that helped poor women with health and child-care issues. It was there she met Sheela Patel who ultimately persuaded her and a few others to come together and create SPARC. The mission of this organization was to partner with the pavement dwellers in order to find solutions that mattered to them, not to provide services and resources that someone else had devised. Subsequently, Celine and the pavement women shared a quarter century of life and work together. They became a family. At the time Celine married, both her parents were deceased. So the women of *Mahila Milan* stepped in as mothers at her wedding, and it was Jockin who gave her away.

I met Celine at the SPARC office in Byculla. It was a small run-down building which looked more like a house than an office. This was the same place where the women would store their valuables and papers when they heard of an impending demolition and where later they displayed the prototype models of their dream homes for others to see.

That day we sat on straw mats and faced each other, sipping small glasses of tea laden with milk and sugar. I took in the row of colorfully clad women, young and old, each a different shape and size. One quietly chewed on beetle nut which had turned her lips bright red; another stared at me curiously as she busily adjusted herself, rocking back and forth until she had found a comfortable sitting position. The smallest one was silver-haired with shriveled hands. Each was decorated in jewelry and radiant patterns.

Celine introduced me to Laxmi, a small, bent woman. I couldn't tell how old she was. Her bronze face was sunken and carved. Brown dry lips embraced an overbite that shone when she smiled; her thinning black hair with grey threads was pulled into a tight knot that revealed ears pierced with gold. Her sari was bright green and royal blue mixed in spiraling rings and draped across her body like a Roman toga. As she stretched it out to cover her crossed legs and leathered feet, the silver bangles on her wrists tinkled against each other. Even the poorest of poor women here rose every morning with adornment.

Laxmi, looked me over with a broad grin, neither shy nor intimidated by my western otherness. The rest of the women eyed me too. After a point they seemed satisfied enough with what they saw and turned their attention to Celine who recounted their story to me.

When Celine was done, the women asked me to tell them about my life. At first I resisted sharing my story. How could I explain what I did to these women? My life was so different than theirs. Then I thought of what Jockin had done so many years before, how he had introduced the sharing of narrative as a way to learn and build community. So I shared the story of The International Forum and how people from all over the world came to learn about how to run their businesses by listening to the experiences of others like them.

Laxmi asked if I measured the impact of what I did in my role at The International Forum. She caught me off guard. I had not given the subject much thought, although based on feedback, I suspected my involvement had a positive effect on people. The old woman was quick to point out that I should know the effect of what I did. Otherwise, how could I be sure I was doing the right thing.

My afternoon with the women of *Mahila Milan* re-inforced for me something I already suspected: even though by conventional standards these women were not "experts," they were exceedingly wise and pragmatic. They also possessed something no development agency had; they were completely vested in the outcome of whatever solution they employed to make their situation better. They understood that whatever route was taken, they would be the ones living with the consequences.

My time in the Mumbai slums with Jockin and others has allowed me to better understand the power of individuals to bring about change. But it is Celine who has helped me see the broader effect that empowering the slum dwellers and pavement dwellers has had on the future of communities and cities around the world. In the years since we first met in Mumbai, she and I have become good friends and she has shared much of what she has learned from her experiences working with the urban poor. For example, when people turn their individual struggles into a collective struggle, they are able to find solutions that they could not have on their own. They are also able to approach those in power, including governments, with one voice and thus, gain their attention. But what gives such a collective credibility is the homework its members do to make a case. Because *Mahila Milan* was able to provide information about who and how many lived in the slums, and in what types of structures, it gained legitimacy with those making decisions and allocating resources. That practice has now been adopted by urban poor in slums all over the world. They provide information that governments need to make intelligent decisions about urban infrastructure and development. Having gained the confidence of the decision-makers, the poor are also designing and developing new community spaces, amenities such as toilet blocks, community meeting places, and sanitation solutions. They have earned a seat at the table for discussions on finding appropriate land and housing solutions for growing urban centers. Instead of being viewed as adversaries or a nuisance, the poor are increasingly becoming partners in the process in many cities. Of course, much work remains to be done before they are viewed as legitimate stakeholders and a key source of valuable information for city planning. Celine continues to work at finding ways for city governments to engage and work with informal communities in order to plan for the future.

Jockin and Celine helped me to understand the critical role that those whom we think we need to help can play in determining and implementing solutions. Devi Shetty said once: "Poor people in isolation are very weak, but together they are very strong." This strength is readily apparent in the network of federations that Jockin helped to create across the world. The power of communities to solve problems in a sustainable way is an untapped resource for all of us. I have no doubt now that society is better served when governments and other large institutions allow stakeholders like *Mahila Milan* to play a role.

Since my visit with *Mahila Milan*, Celine has kept me apprised of its progress. In 2014, the pavement dwellers were finally granted the land they so relentlessly sought for over twenty years. With the money they saved and the house designs they made, they left the pavement for good and moved to a new community. Eighty families were part of the first wave, and many more have followed.

The plans for redeveloping Dharavi, that had been occupying so much of Jockin's attention when I last visited him, have since been delayed several times. The consultant in charge of the project, who was promoting a top-down approach, has been relieved of his position. Financial issues and corruption charges have further hindered progress. But the slum dwellers' agenda remains firm and has become an integral part of the ongoing dialogue and negotiations. The redevelopment of Dharavi will happen at some point. Its fairness—and success—will, in my opinion, depend on the extent to which the powers-that-be adopt a bottom-up approach that incorporates all stakeholders.

Although my visits to Mumbai showed me the power of communities to solve their own challenges in ways that neither individual, experts, or institutions, ever could, visits elsewhere demonstrated that barriers to such an approach remain. In fact, there are some in the world who will go out of their way to ensure that problems are never solved this way. Case in point: the story of Nancy Harris and the Terma Foundation.

The Warrior

Pain insists upon being attended to.

God whispers to us in our pleasures,

speaks in our consciences, but shouts in our pains.

It is his megaphone to rouse a deaf world.

– C.S. LEWIS

Nancy Harris

Dr. Nancy Harris remembers the day the Dalai Lama came to thank her, because when His Holiness put her hand in his, she knew without a doubt what her purpose in life was going to be. She would take all that she knew, and all that she had, and devote herself to stopping the suffering she had seen.

The year was 1990 and she was in Dharamsala. She had just finished working triage for three months in a refugee camp in Nepal and was preparting to return home. This was her final stop on a year-long journey which had started in Beijing, then taken her to Tibet, and then to India. While she was in Delhi, she had met a member of the Tibetan Community in Exile who had asked for her medical assistance in treating the sick Tibetans who were arriving in droves from China. Nancy agreed to help, delaying her departure home.

A self-professed workaholic since the age of five, Nancy had graduated from Yale University, received a Fulbright Scholarship, and then put herself through Stanford Medical School. Following her residency she served three grueling years in the National Health Services Corps to pay off her debts. She then worked in an emergency room and took on various jobs working in AIDS clinics to build a nest egg that would allow her to make choices in her life. Initially she expected she would settle in California and practice but that did not happen. At the age of thirty-three, Nancy left the U.S. and went to Beijing to study Traditional Chinese Medicine, an alternative approach to everything she had learned in her Western training.

Through people she knew, she secured a visa to travel to Tibet, a place about which she knew little but was curious to see. Once there, she travelled alone across the Tibetan Plateau from Lhasa to Everest and back. Along the way she could not help but notice the stunted size of the children she met in the villages. Something wasn't right. Upon her return to the capital city, she learned of a study done by UNICEF that had concluded that high altitudes hindered physical development. She didn't believe it. While on a Fullbright Scholarship in Chile she had encountered many children living at high altitudes. They had not exhibited any of the physical stunting she had observed in the Tibetan children. There must be another explanation and she wanted to know what it was. Nancy had been given the name of a local doctor in Lhasa by a fellow student whom she had met in Beijing. She found the doctor and shared with him her concerns. He listened and agreed to help her uncover what was ailing the children. When Nancy left Lhasa, she had every intention of returning just as soon as she could secure financial support to begin research. However, it would take three more years to get the permission she needed from the Chinese government to return to

Tibet and begin her investigation. That was more than twenty-five years ago.

"They say that medicine is a science and not an art, but it's not true," Nancy says. "There are things happening with the human organism that we don't fully understand. There are people who shouldn't have died and did. And there are others who haven't died and should have. Back then I was trying to make sense of all of this based on my scientific training. But I couldn't."

It is late afternoon in California and the sun is shining down through the divided skylight in her home. Nancy carefully places a photo of her and the Dalai Lama back on the shelf where it belongs. The kitchen behind her is empty and spotless; the countertops barren, and the appliances new and unused. It is as if everything is being saved for when she decides to live here full time; when she is no longer travelling back and forth across the world to save people; when and if that day ever comes.

The strain of the life she has chosen has left its mark. Nancy's face is weathered. Her blond hair, streaked with grey, is carelessly drawn into a knot. She wears a clean light green zip hooded sweatshirt, the type a teenager might wear, not an Ivy League-educated doctor. Her only adornment is a simple gold chain around her white neck and small hoop earrings. There is nothing that is memorable about her appearance except her eyes. In contrast to the deliberateness with which she moves, her deep set, grey eyes emanate energy. She uses them purposefully; watching everything and everyone.

Nancy considers herself a warrior, a fighter and a survivor. But the human suffering she has seen and experienced have taken their toll. Her father, who supported and believed in her through the first half of her life, died while Nancy was still in school. She says that in some ways she still hasn't recovered from the loss.

"Back then I was determined to understand not only my own suffering, but also human suffering. I had no way to explain it to myself outside of a medical or theology framework. I needed to know where to hang all the sorrow and pain, disaster and horrible deaths I had seen," she says.

The deep crease that intersects her brow and the tight line of her mouth hint at the frustration she is feeling now. She has been home in California this time for longer than she planned because the Chinese government has twice denied her request for a visa to go back to Tibet. The word from people she knows there is that she may not be welcome anymore. She is worried that after almost three decades of working to cure over one million Tibetans of malnutrition and tuberculosis, she may never be allowed to return.

It is unclear what put her on the blacklist this time. Perhaps it was the article about her work written by a well-meaning journalist in China that went viral on the internet. The publicity may not have been welcomed by someone with power. Or maybe she angered the wrong government official by doing something that was good but made him look bad; it would not be the first time. The real reasons behind the setbacks and betrayals she has experienced over the years working in Tibet have always been opaque. But unlike now, she was always allowed to return when things died down.

In the beginning it was easier; there were more people on her side. But circumstances changed as leadership changed. In 1993, the Chinese government finally gave Nancy permission along with a team of Chinese, Tibetans, and Westerners to investigate the health condition of the children of Tibet. Was altitude the cause of the problems, or as Nancy had suspected on her first visit, were there other factors? "Everyone said I was crazy to go back to Tibet and that I could never accomplish what I wanted to. I am glad I didn't listen to them," she says.

She remembers being moved by the urgency with which the parents and grandparents wanted to have the children measured and tested. They knew that something was dreadfully wrong. As Nancy unwound the layers of their swaddled children, she was shocked at the distended stomachs, and emaciated arms and legs. Many had blond hair, not a genetic trait but rather an indication of serious protein deficiencies.

The team worked ten hours measuring and examining fifty to one hundred children a day in villages all across the Plateau. What they discovered was a severely malnourished population, a condition that had presented itself within the previous fifty years. As early as the first year of life, the size of a child fell rapidly below the world average. By the age of five, they could never catch up. The results of Nancy's research indicated that 71% of the children suffered from intestinal parasites, 41% had chronic malnutrition, and 67% had rickets. Disease patterns often followed geography, as some parts of Tibet were richer in certain minerals than others. In the east the people were taller because the land was more fertile, but even there the team found indications of child malnutrition and disease. In 1994, Nancy published her findings in the *New England Journal of Medicine*.

Her work evolved quickly from research to care and treatment. Initially, she funded her research with her own savings, but she needed more if she was going to start treating patients. She returned to the U.S. to raise money but it was not easy. Medical schools do not teach fundraising.

"My training was in tertiary care. I did not know one thing about public health or running a non-government organization," she says.

She approached a number of foundations for money and was turned down again and again. Eventually one individual wrote a check for $30,000 and Nancy created the Terma Foundation. The word *Terma* in Buddhist texts means "hidden treasure." Literally it refers to items or books that were buried at one time in history to preserve them from harm or destruction. But more often Terma refers to the wisdom that is in the mind of a guru that remains hidden until it is the right time to teach it or until a student is ready to receive it.

Back in Tibet, Nancy built a network on the ground of doctors, volunteers and healthcare workers who had knowlege that the population needed. The mission of Terma was to help educate people, to share information and teach others how to identify and prevent illness and disease. In addition to distributing over one million imported vitamins and supplements each year, Nancy worked to revive traditional health practices and food strategies that the Tibetans had lost under Chinese occupation. She re-introduced more vegetables, tubers and high protein plant foods into their diet. She also started a campaign to teach the importance of hand washing using soap.

"Tibetans lost a whole generation who had the know-how to survive," says Nancy. During the Cultural Revolution in the 1960s, many of Tibet's written records were destroyed and those with the knowledge of how to survive were killed. Then government-imposed practices of mono-cropping and bio-chemical fertilizers depleted the soil of necessary minerals and nutrients. As a result, malnutrition became an epidemic.

"The filth, the garbage, the prostitution that you see now was not there before. The old Tibetans tell me they had hot water when they were young, they kept clean, they washed their hands, they used the sun for vitamins," she says. "But good health requires knowledge."

Today a large part of sustainable development in the world is about what she calls *medical imperialism*—ideas that have been proven to work elsewhere and are then brought by experts to bear on a new situation. Nancy thinks there is a better way.

"What it involves is listening for a long time and observing. Before proposing things, you have to understand what people within that culture perceive their needs to be," she says. "For example, how does one teach someone who does not know what a germ is, the importance of hand washing?"

Through conversations and observations Nancy knew that the Tibetans understood that eyeglasses enabled them to see smaller and smaller things. She showed them that with a microscope they could see something as small as a germ. Because they already believed that invisible worlds exist all around them and that when energies go out of balance unpleasant things occur, the concept of a germ was understandable.

"You can make adaptations to behavior without making them anti-cultural or disparaging of the tradition," she says. "There are certain cultural belief systems that we were able to tap into once we understood them."

Whenever she was in Lhasa Nancy saw patients at the Terma clinic. She treated up to a hundred people a day. For several months a year, she travelled with her team along treacherous roads to help those who were ill, while also connecting with others who would carry their effort further. She remembers one trip when their car got stuck in a mudslide and rocks were falling all around them. They were almost crushed and killed. It took them three days to get free.

Nancy has never worked alone. "Basically anyone whose lights were on, we talked into joining the effort. And whatever worked we tried; because nothing had worked before. I think that was our brilliance," she says.

Not so brilliant was the bureaucracy they faced. It took a frustrating six months to negotiate access to an area in order to treat people. Then the next year negotiations had to begin anew. Even worse, medicine and supplies were constantly confiscated by customs officials under the guise of paperwork not being filed correctly.

Nancy's right hand person in Tibet is a Belgian woman named Françoise Begaux. They met when Françoise was working for a large global health organization. When her employer pulled out of Tibet, she joined Nancy's team.

"Nancy came to Tibet for one reason. She came simply to save lives," says Françoise. "When I met her I wondered how she could do all this by herself. She created the program, she got the money, she dealt with the authorities, she published articles, and she hired and fired staff. I had been spoiled. I had someone to look after my health benefits, my retirement and all my things from Brussels."

Nancy and her team had suspected the presence of tuberculosis (TB) in the population for some time. But it was a routine x-ray of a child with rickets in 2000 that confirmed it and led the Terma crew to take on one of the biggest killers in the world today.

Tuberculosis is one of the most prevalent diseases. A third of humanity carries the bacteria, though not all are actually afflicted with the ailment. Nevertheless, about nine million people a year become sick with it, and two million die. Tragically, only one-third of those who contract the disease ever receive treatment. Most victims die because they are too hard to reach, do not know they have it, or do not have access to proper healthcare. A person who is sick with TB will infect ten to fifteen people a year if left untreated. Today about 40% of AIDS related deaths are caused by TB because the bacteria are so prevalent, especially among poor and marginalized populations.

In Tibet, basic TB was becoming an epidemic and new strains of drug-resistant TB had already presented in the population. Multiple Drug Resistant (MDR) and Extensively Drug Resistant (X-MDR) Tuberculosis are mutations that have developed because patients have not completed treatment and thus allow the bacterium to survive, change and adapt. Education is the biggest weapon against the spread of MDR TB because unlike basic TB, once a patient contracts a drug-resistant strain it is almost too late. Treatment takes much longer and costs five hundred times what it does for basic TB.

Nancy worried that TB in Tibet was far more prevalent than reported. State hospitals had been designated specifically to treat the disease, but were sorely deficient in supplies and expertise. A medical tidal wave was quietly building.

In China, a patient must get a diagnosis from a TB hospital in order to receive state-funded treatment. But there are few such hospitals in the province, and there is only one in the Tibetan capital, Lhasa. This has created a severe bottleneck. Nancy estimated at least 6,000 new cases a year in the eastern prefecture of Chamdo alone, but the TB hospital there has resources to handle only 200. A sick villager must give up days of work and walk an average of forty miles for treatment. As a result, most don't seek help.

In the past fifteen years, Terma has expanded the alternatives for diagnosis and care in Tibet, but there is much more work to be done. "We work with the county doctors because they are really committed and easy to work with," says Françoise. "One of the problems in China is that people who are in responsible positions change so frequently and the new person doesn't like what the old person did. There are a lot of NGOs in Tibet training and teaching, but there are almost none working with primary care and none are dealing with TB. I've seen so many people die. I've held the hand of so many as they die. It is suffocating, it is ugly. And no one hears them. We are their voice."

Nancy tells the story of Daka Droma, a twenty-four-year old girl who was the pride of her middle class Lhasa family. Her parents used their savings to send her away to law school in Kunming. During her third year there she fell ill. Alone in her dormitory, she became very weak and lost weight. Eventually the university discovered her condition and sent her home, where she was diagnosed with advanced contagious pulmonary TB. The disease had spread to other parts of her body. She was admitted to the local hospital and remained there for three months, but did not improve. Eventually she was discharged. She had lost close to half of her body weight.

Nancy learned of her condition when the family could no longer afford the medical bills. The Terma Foundation paid for her hospital stay. Nancy took over her care and provided medicine and oxygen. She taught the family about nutritional rehabilitation and pain abatement. The family created separate living quarters for Daka so that the disease would not spread to others. There she was cared for peacefully and visited regularly by Nancy.

As the days passed, her condition worsened. The tuberculosis, which had started in the lungs, had moved to her abdomen. Her stomach was bloated and stained a dark purple. Movement was very painful, but the oxygen made the symptoms easier to bear. Her extremities, ankles and feet were swollen and she suffered acute bed sores. Nancy touched the young woman whenever she spoke to her, and reassured and encouraged her. She did the same for her family while also giving them room to grieve. Daka Droma did not survive. Sadly, she could have been cured if diagnosed early and treated properly.

"In this day and age TB is entirely preventable. If they would just let us do our work here we could cure people for only $40," says Nancy. She is referring to the Health Department in Tibet, whose members for the most part are untrained and corrupt. "When they get money they spend it on Land Cruisers. They aren't using it for TB."

In an effort to get out in front of the epidemic and stop further cases like Daka Droma's, Nancy developed a network of mobile healthcare workers at the grassroots to identify and treat patients. She also trained teachers, community leaders and others to manage patient recovery and to ensure that medicine was taken properly and to completion. Since 90% of TB patients don't experience complications once treatment begins, oversight can be carried out by trained non-medical people such as family members or neighbors.

One of Terma's most effective programs has been the TB Ambassadors. People who have been cured by Terma are expected to go back to their village and share with others how TB is transmitted, diagnosed and where to get medicine. Those who have had the disease are more successful even than most medical personnel at identifying people who are infected. People suspected of having TB are then taken by truck to Nancy in Lhasa or to the local TB hospital for official diagnosis and treatment. These Ambassadors have become the eyes and ears of Nancy's effort across Tibet.

Because most medicines available in Tibet are either of poor quality or fake, Terma offers patients the option to switch the TB medicine they receive at a government hospital for Western medicine. Nancy devotes a significant amount of time to ensuring a regular supply is brought in from outside China and makes it through the onerous customs process. Even so, shipments regularly get held up, are subject to huge fines and get confiscated. Then the same medicine shows up in the local TB hospitals after someone has re-sold it for a profit.

For those patients who are clearly infected with TB but cannot be officially diagnosed by a sputum test, Terma offers free x-rays. TB can afflict many other parts of the body including bones, brain, kidneys, and reproductive organs. Nancy has successfully lobbied Beijing for a change in policy, so that patients with extra pulmonary TB can get free x-rays and have their treatment paid for by the state. Before this thousands went undiagnosed.

The Terma Foundation has become the primary, if not the only, advocate for accessible healthcare for the Tibetan people to both the Chinese government and the World Health Organization. Nancy and her team have treated more than 200,000 patients and saved over one million lives through education programs, nutrition strategies, new hygiene practices, and distribution of medicine and supplements. Most of their programs are so well ingrained in the communities and villages that even when Nancy is absent, the work continues. She is now planning for the day when she no longer has to be in Tibet throughout the year. She feels it is time to direct her attention to other countries in need.

"We have talked about handing over what we have put in place to the Tibetans to run, and I've met with the Dalai Lama's health minister to discuss this," she says. They are so busy, however, that it remains unclear how this might be done.

Because Nancy has not been allowed to return to China, this transition may happen sooner than she expected. Without her there, patients who go to the hospitals will be turned away and the disease will keep spreading.

"It really matters what happens in Tibet. There are six million Tibetans in China and only 150,000 outside the country. The future of Tibetans in China will dictate the future of Tibetans globally," she says.

It is tempting to become discouraged. Nancy has her dark days. But, she says,

"When I talk to other doctors I know here in the U.S., they cannot wait to get out of it, to retire and collect their pension. Then I realize how fortunate I am that I have been able to fulfill the moral and professional point of why I became a doctor."

In the corner of her room a short set of stairs run to a mezzanine. On it is a desk, a phone, a computer and a long window that overlooks the Pacific Ocean. She has bills to pay, paperwork due to the IRS and in a few hours she will be on the phone to her team in Lhasa or to her donors in Europe. For now, however, she contemplates the view of the setting sun.

"I never doubted what I was doing and I know that the bad feelings will cycle out and I will find strength again."

As she considers all that has been accomplished in the past quarter century, she cannot believe that such a small group of people, most of who had no formal healthcare training, was actually responsible for it all. "We really moved mountains. I think it will have lasting benefits. But it may be that in the end what happens will have nothing to do with me. It may be that the Tibetans won't make it; they have been very complicit in their own tragedy. But if all that was humanly possible was done in extending a hand to them, then we certainly did our best at that." ✸

Lhasa, Tibet _____

I first met Nancy in Lhasa in 2004. At the time I was leading a group on an extended trip to Tibet following one of our programs in China. I was introduced to her by an American guide I knew. Nancy felt it important that before we talked about her work I should experience it for myself, so she arranged for me to accompany Françoise the next day to one of the villages.

It was bitter cold when we carried bags of supplies from the van to a courtyard in the middle of the village. The Himalayan winds whipped against the roofs of the surrounding huts, lifting strings of prayer flags into colorful arcs over our heads. We were fortunate that the tall whitewashed walls that enclosed the yard protected us as we pinned bolts of red cloth with photographs and drawings that told stories of children being stalked by ugly germ monsters who were ultimately slain by hand-washers. Some villagers crowded in to watch. Others stepped forward to help, grabbing corners of the banners in their dry, cracked fingers. Tying them with string, they wrapped the cloth around scarred and bleached poles that had once been feeble trees.

The gathering grew. Old men in felt-brimmed hats and layers of coats covered with dust, grandmothers with plaid wool scarves wrapped around their heads and well-worn striped aprons appeared. Their daughters sported a variety of dirty hats and sweaters that looked as if they didn't quite fit. They balanced their smallest children on their hips. A grandfather with a red scarf wrapped around his head carried his grandson strapped to his back with a long pink sash. They had come to welcome us, but also to collect soap, vitamins, medicine, get a checkup, and to socialize.

I remember feeling a tug on my jacket and looking down into the grubby face of a little boy. He raised his hand and a rough, sticky paw wiggled in between my fingers. Then he pulled me towards a sagging earthen building and through a short doorway. Inside, I saw a young woman from the Terma team next to a long, low lamp. A dim blue light reflected off her fleece lined quilted vest. The rest of her body had been swallowed up by the blackness. The boy let go of me and stepped towards her. With palms open, he thrust his hands under the blue light. Then he turned to me chattering.

"He wants to show you the dirt on his hands," said the woman. I looked down.

"The bacteria show up as white patches on his skin under this light. He knows that those are germs and germs make people sick." The little paws were filthy.

Then the boy took my hand, drawing it towards the light. I leaned in. We both saw that big white blotchy germ patches covered my palms as well. We laughed. Then I got a lecture.

"He says you need to wash your hands," the woman translated.

I certainly did.

Back outside, I found Françoise examining a small child. Her fingers parted the hair on his head so she could note pigment changes. She touched his face, his rough red cheeks and looked into his eyes. He opened his mouth, and she examined his tongue and throat. Then she lifted him onto an old white bathroom scale to see if he had gained weight since her last visit. The child's mother and father stood by watching while a young man who also worked for Terma translated what Françoise was saying.

For more than two decades this team had tackled challenges that more seasoned agencies around the world would not dare touch. They returned often to the villages to see if what they had put in place was working. Were people washing their hands, using soap, taking vitamins, exposing their babies to sun and separating drinking water from waste? Were those infected with TB taking their medicine, maintaining well-ventilated living spaces, not spitting or doing anything which might spread their infection to others?

"I like going back to the villages," said Françoise. "You have to keep going back to be sure that what you are doing is working and also to learn from your mistakes."

When our work was done, we returned to Lhasa and I sat down for a conversation with Nancy. My impression of her then was of a tough, cool, and guarded woman who had been living in China for too long. It was as if the corruption, red tape and inefficiencies had got to her. I remember thinking she was far too impatient to be effective in a place where it took ten times longer to get something done if it got done at all.

In time, however, I modified my view as I learned how skillfully she had managed the grey zone and developed an understanding of what motivated the people with whom she had to negotiate. Terma was not an officially registered organization in China and Nancy had no interest in it becoming one. "I don't want the stamp," she had said. "I want the relationships." She cultivated those well. She understood the power of leverage and how badly many of the officials whom she knew wanted, among other things, that their child have access to American universities. Nancy could offer that access through people she knew. Ultimately she found the balance between impatience and patience, and she used that to the benefit of her work.

After I left Lhasa it was almost four years before I saw Nancy at her home in California —when she was, as she put it, "in exile." When I left she was planning to travel to Thailand. There, she expected to have better luck getting a visa for China, she told me.

Six months later when I arrived in Bangkok to meet another of my subjects, Mechai Viravaidya, Nancy was still there. In spite of failing once again to return to Tibet, she had no intention of giving up. She was still that warrior woman she had once referred to herself as. Meanwhile Françoise had been allowed to return, and Terma's work was continuing under her leadership.

After Bangkok I didn't see Nancy again, but I received periodic updates of her progress. Terma's work continued in Tibet through new partnerships with U.S. and Chinese charities though it is unclear to me if Nancy herself ever returned. She was able to re-direct her attention to new regions and she expanded the geographic scope of

Terma by launching new programs in Burma and Brazil. The TB Ambassador Program is now being implemented in the Favelas of Rio de Janeiro.

My experiences with Nancy generated a number of themes upon which I was able to build as I moved forward and learned from others. Terma's success reinforced for me the importance of uncovering answers that are truly relevant to the people one is trying to help. I had already learned this from Jockin and Lily, but nowhere is this more critical than in a place like Tibet where at any moment access to the rest of the world and its resources may be cut off. Solutions to challenges there have to be self-sustaining.

"Often the best solutions are not the ones that worked somewhere else in the world and are then imposed upon a situation from the top down," said Nancy. "Rather the most sustainable approaches are ones that come from understanding the culture and then creating health solutions from within that culture."

This is exactly what Terma had done in Tibet and what made its approach both unique and longer lasting than others in spite of the obstacles.

Nancy also understood something that I would learn more about later. She knew that every person has strengths which once identified and encouraged can help to solve problems. Regardless of education or economics, anyone can play a role in making things better. Perhaps because her resources were so limited, Nancy had no choice but to work with what and who she had available to her. Had she been well-funded and well-supported, she may never have made this discovery.

I also learned something about what motivates someone like

Nancy to walk away from an opportunity to be a successful doctor in a "developed" country and instead treat people on the other side of the world who could never pay her. At face value it seemed like career suicide, not to mention a risk to both her personal safety as well as her long term well-being. Why did she do it? And what made her think that she could succeed?

"You had the whole world in front of you after graduating from two top schools with excellent credentials. So why did you do it when you could have gone on to be a famous, financially successful doctor in the U.S.?" I asked.

"To a very large part of the world, I am a famous doctor," she said. "But it is not about fame anyway. The minute *what* you do becomes *about* you, you become entangled and confused and misdirected. Ego kills altruism."

I thought of all the egos involved in altruistic missions around the world. Is it possible they could be slowly killing the very efforts they were supposed to support?

What surprised me about Nancy was that she didn't intended to accomplish all that she did. She had no grand vision for the end-game. In the beginning she didn't even have a plan. She just took a chance to research and write about a problem she saw while travelling in a country about which she knew very little. Then one thing led to another and twenty-five years later, she turned around and couldn't believe what they had all accomplished.

I once asked her if she could have anything, what it would be. Money, surprisingly, was not the first thing she listed, though I know it is a constant struggle for her to raise funds. Rather what she wanted most was the encouragement, the counsel and the feedback of others who like her were working at the grassroots to make thing better somewhere in the world. She wanted to talk with them about the challenges that they faced and what they had done about them. She wanted to learn so she could do what she was already doing, better.

With this in mind, I connected Nancy with a man in Bangkok, who for decades had been adopting best-practices from business, healthcare, education, and other disciplines in an effort to enrich the lives and livelihoods of his countrymen.

The Entrepreneur

Ultimately humanity is one, and this small planet is our only home. If we are to protect this home of ours, each of us needs to experience a vivid sense of universal altruism. It is only this feeling that can remove the self-centered motives that cause people to deceive and misuse one another – I believe that at every level of society – familial, tribal, national and international - the key to a happier and more successful world is the growth of compassion. We do not need to become more religious, nor do we need to believe in ideology. All that is necessary is for each of us to develop our good human qualities.

– HIS HOLINESS, THE DALAI LAMA

Mechai Viravaidya

Mechai Viravaidya is tall, trim, and neatly pressed into a pair of smart, lightweight charcoal trousers and a white-collared camp shirt. His wire-rimmed glasses magnify his large black eyes, which dart back and forth taking in the chaos building around him. He once had a decent head of hair, but in the past ten years it has gradually thinned into patches of grey and black. He is polite, but cool, as he shakes hands in the gathering crowd.

It is hard to imagine that this rather proper gentleman in his mid-seventies is the same man who introduced the birth control pill to his procreative countrymen in an effort to curb a population explosion; the same man who brought the condom to prostitutes and their clients in the red light district in Bangkok in the middle of an AIDS epidemic. It is equally difficult to imagine that while holding various positions in the government, leading businesses, and writing a newspaper column on economics and development,

Mechai also managed to build an organization that helped to bring better healthcare to the poor, offer financial and business support to rural entrepreneurs, ensure that environmental sustainability was an integral part of any plan to develop rural livelihoods, and now devotes his time to creating a brand new model for educating rural youth.

Today Mechai looks more like a gentle grandfather than the upstart "Condom King" as he was called in the 1990s. But he is the same man who, upon learning that people were repulsed by the idea of using a condom, assured them it was nothing more than a product from a tree with universal applications; the sturdy ring at its base could be used to tie up your hair, and the lubricant used to grease a rusty hinge. In spite of his stoic expression today, he is a man who liked to have fun — and still does.

It is mid-morning and already over one hundred degrees in the shade. The sun beats brutally on the red earth in this northeast corner of Thailand, not far from the Cambodian border. Mechai is surrounded by teachers who have come to have their picture taken with him. Six years ago, the Pattana Primary School opened its doors in one of the poorest regions of this country. Today a new secondary school is being launched. These schools were Mechai's idea, the latest projects in his over forty-year crusade to economically empower the rural poor.

He stands patiently as the chaos settles around him. He spares a few words for the adults nearby and then turns his attention to the children. They are coming towards him in their new school uniforms – white collared shirts with plaid piping on top of dark blue skirts and pants. The girls' hair has been pulled back by a mother's hand; the boys' is combed. As the students get closer, Mechai's expression relaxes into a broad smile.

Someone asks to take their picture. Mechai organizes the children, stands behind them, and a photographer captures the moment. Once the photo is taken the students run off in twos and threes towards the collection of buildings ahead.

The new secondary school has been built as a community of small huts around a central pavilion. Each has a peaked green metal roof, Thai style, with large overhangs to protect the interior from sudden downpours. The walls have been constructed from bamboo and are open on all sides like a Balinese home where air flows freely between the space inside and the elements outside.

The design for these was inspired by *Rubanisation*, or the creation of autonomously functioning communities set in the natural world, which support livelihoods, education, communication and transportation. The architect for the secondary school was a Singaporean who is rethinking the way people exist together and how place and space can create conditions that help improve the way people live.

The Pattana School is surrounded by fields of growing vegetables. They are used as a live classroom not only for the students, but also for parents who are involved in seeding, cultivating and harvesting. The fresh vegetables are incorporated into the school meals and what is left over is sold in local markets. The proceeds help to pay for the operations of the school.

Mechai explains: "The money to build the primary school came from a donation. For the secondary school I put money into it myself along with some from the Gates Foundation. The next step will be to establish a company whose profits will be used to run it going forward."

All of Mechai's previous projects were self-funded either through their own revenue generating activities or from the profits of companies that have been created explicitly to support them. Mechai calls these entities *businesses with a social purpose.* "The first company we set up was a clinic that distributed contraceptives, then a restaurant, then more restaurants and then a resort," he says.

Eighteen different businesses with a social purpose currently fund the Population and Community Development Association (PDA), the organization which Mechai founded in 1974. PDA was originally created to help promote family planning in Thailand, but over the years its mission crept to include health, sanitation, income generation, poverty eradication, environment sustainability, and now education and schools.

Mechai maintains that our ability to alleviate poverty in the world has been limited. Despite good intentions, government efforts have fallen short, and private philanthropy just isn't robust enough to support every initiative. If, however, you can establish a business to fund your NGO, it is much easier to sustain your effort, says Mechai. You are not dependent on donors, and at the same time because you are able to fund yourself, you are much more attractive to them. Mechai is the first to admit this is not always a viable option. Thus, he is constantly seeking new ways to sustain his grassroots efforts.

"It is a fallacy to believe that government can solve everything," he says. "There are shortcomings everywhere in government, in the marketplace. So I ask everyone to help us – banks, companies, individuals. I used to chair a petroleum company (I have a little business in my background). I got them to sell seed at their gas stations. Everyone knows where the gas station is, but they do not always know where the seed or agriculture store is. We need to think out of the box if we are going to solve problems in the future."

Mechai did not come from a village like those where he now spends his time. He is the grandson of Phraya Damrong Paetayakhun, a commoner who rose to the rank of Major General, Army Surgeon General, and personal physician to the Queen Mother in the early part of the 20th century. The King gave Mechai's grandfather the surname "Viravaidya," meaning "brave doctor." The honor bestowed status as well as property to Mechai's family.

Mechai grew up in a culturally mixed household. His father was Thai, his mother Scottish. They were both doctors. Mechai was the eldest of four children.

As a young man Mechai studied to be an economist, not a social entrepreneur. In the late 1960s, he was employed by a government agency coordinating the vast amount of foreign economic aid being poured into Thailand. While working on infrastructure projects in rural areas, he noticed poor families struggling to feed seven to ten children. "I saw that everything was supposed to be done for the people, but the people were never involved," he says.

While working for the government, Mechai also taught English in the evening, had a radio program at night, and wrote a column on economic development. "I learned a lot that way and earned extra money," he says. It also enabled him to forge connections and relationships that would aid him later in his work.

In the 1970s, Thailand was facing two serious problems: poverty and a population explosion. The population was growing at over 3%, or two million people a year. The government had tried for a decade to lower fertility rates, with little success. If the country was going to realize the benefits of economic development, its population had to stop growing. But societal taboos about sex and contraceptives had made this a subject few would discuss.

Mechai believed that if people could talk openly about these matters, they could address the problem. When he was offered a job with The Planned Parenthood Association of Thailand, he saw a chance to do something and left his job in development. With Planned Parenthood behind him, he re-named the birth control pill the *Family Welfare Vitamin* and launched a campaign to promote it. *"Mothers take it for the health of the family,"* was one of his sayings.

He also introduced the condom to Thai society, creating catch phrases and tag lines to make the subject less intimidating, such as: *"Too many children make you poor,"* and *"A condom a day keeps the doctor away."* He promoted vasectomies as another option for birth control with slogans such as: *"Bring your dad in for a Father's Day Vasectomy - If you don't want to dilute your inheritance."* And, he organized events such as the July 4th Vasectomy Festival. The procedure was performed across the street from the American Embassy in Bangkok. *"Walk in and get it over with, then have a hot dog for lunch,"* proclaimed the literature.

The birth control pill however presented problems. The Thai people accepted the pill, but it was limited in its distribution and availability. As in the West, it had to be prescribed by a medical doctor. In Thailand there was one doctor for every one hundred thousand women, and most of the doctors were in clinics and medical centers in cities, too far away for a poor villager to spare a day's work to visit.

Mechai proposed distributing the pills through nurses and midwives and other trained people in the villages. The government initially said no. But Mechai persisted and was able to convince the Royal College of General Physicians to agree that non-physicians who were carefully managed could administer the pill. Hair dressers, teachers and other volunteers were trained. They kept a portion of each sale they made; the balance went to supporting community-based distribution programs and the training of new sales staff.

"Even back then, though we were in the nonprofit world, we did cost *recovery*. The people who took the *Family Welfare Vitamin* paid for it over a five year period. No one got it for free. We were already starting to be self-sustaining," Mechai says.

The distribution of the *Family Welfare Vitamin* had the desired effect. By 1994 the population growth rate in Thailand had fallen from 3.3% to 1.2% and in 2006 it dropped to 0.5%.

Several PDA employees have made the trip up from Bangkok with Mechai for the school opening. As their leader winds his way across the red earth towards one of the classroom buildings, they fall in step behind him. The team is a mix of young Thais and a few foreigners. The woman who manages public relations for PDA worked in advertising before going to the U.S. to study for her Executive MBA. When she returned to Thailand she became a public relations consultant. She knew Mechai for years before she agreed to come and work for him. She appreciates his willingness to give employees a great deal of autonomy. He provides direction at the beginning of a project and finishing touches at the end, but leaves implementation to others.

Working for Mechai can at times be a bit chaotic, say those on his team. Everywhere he goes, he observes and takes in new ideas. The team is accustomed to being told to *"write that down,"* so they come prepared with pen and paper. He is also an avid reader but he does not have time to read all the books he wants. So he assigns some to his close advisors and asks them to return with a summary. Rather than struggle to use his iPhone he will hand it to someone else to figure out. He does, however, read every e-mail that comes across his desk.

In the late 1980s AIDS overtook Thailand, but the government was slow to respond. Mechai, who had grown familiar with all things sexual in Thai society, stepped in. He faced several obstacles when he launched his first anti-AIDS campaign. The powers-that-be did not want to publicize the epidemic because it had the potential to destroy the tourism industry. In addition, several members in the government owned brothels in Bangkok's red light district and profited from its renowned sex trade.

Much to the embarrassment of some of his family members, Mechai took to the streets and asked Thais to unite against the disease. He and his team blew up condoms like balloons and handed out information about AIDS. When it became evident that many in the army were infected, the head of the military finally asked for Mechai's support.

Following a coup in 1991, the interim Prime Minister, who knew Mechai personally, appointed him Minister of Mass Communication with the added responsibility for National AIDS Prevention and Control. Mechai persisted in his effort to fight the spread of the disease. His place in Thai society afforded him some latitude, but his antics also made him an outsider. He didn't care. "My mother once said that if people like you who are educated don't help others, then who will," he says.

In the 1990s Thailand became the only Asian country to successfully curb the spread of AIDS. It is estimated that over seven million Thais were saved because of the work of PDA. The word for condom in the Thai language is "mechai".

Today Mechai's attention is on the children and on a foundation that he has established in part with the sale of land left to him by his father. Over the years, Mechai balanced the running of PDA with other jobs he held in business and government, but he has finally handed leadership of it to a new generation.

"If I drop dead tomorrow, I will not be able to tell them what to do. So they are on their own now. Can they innovate? If they can't they will become a museum or a cemetery. If you cannot keep thinking of new ideas you should go away."

Mechai approaches one of the new classroom huts. Through the gaps created by the walls of bamboo, he catches a glimpse of the large display boards, low lying tables, and the shadows of young forms moving about. The students are preparing to show the work they have completed.

"This is very interesting," Mechai says as he steps inside and moves in front of a collection of hand drawn diagrams. *How can I take care of the world?*, it says. And *if I had a million dollars what would I do? ...waste management, planting trees, prevent burning activities, reuse whatever can be used, and tell other people what to do to reduce consumption of electricity.* His eyes widen behind his glasses as he leans in to get a better look. "These questions make young brains work."

A row of tall glass bottles containing different intensities of yellow liquid rests on a nearby table. "This is a sample of bio-diesel that they have learned to make, and it is now used to power the school tractor," he says.

Sustainability is key. That tractor harvests the adjacent fields. And profits from the harvest support the school.

Mechai has incorporated the natural world into almost everything PDA does. Most of what we need to survive can be found in nature already, and the sustainability of the earth's resources is our primary weapon to fight poverty, he explains.

Understanding who the poor are and what they are capable of is less obvious, but an equally important weapon. "A lot of people mean well when they try to help, but often what they do only makes the poor dependent on hand outs. Whether it is picking up garbage or selling food, they are all engaged in trying to make money to live. But many fail because they don't have the skills to run a business, and most importantly, they don't have access to credit. It should be a human right to get credit." Mechai says. "The only route out of poverty is business."

Not far from the Pattana School is PDA's Nan Rong Center. It is one of eighteen in Thailand from which Mechai's team works. Initially PDA had relationships with 18,000 of Thailand's 60,000 villages through family planning initiatives. Its Village Development Partnership (VDP) focuses on one thousand of these.

The VDP has been responsible for seeding many of the small businesses nearby, including a lemon farm run by family members of the students from the school, an organic fertilizing business which supports local growers and produces excess to sell to markets, a shirt factory, a dried pork producer, mushroom and frog farms, and a weaving and textile workshop. VDP has also helped to finance a rice mill, a community center with computers to access real time market information for selling products, coursework to learn accounting and business skills, and a village library.

VDP supports a bottom up, not top down, approach. The villagers, not outside "experts," take responsibility for identifying their priorities.

This effort requires a strong social framework through which the villagers can agree on their needs, make decisions, plan, and measure their progress. A group of people are selected from among them to spearhead the wish list, visit other communities in other parts of the country to see what works, and collaborate with outside resources to make it happen.

By the time a funder of a Village Development Partnership project arrives with check book in hand, the villagers have already prioritized their needs and have the structure in place to implement. Mechai draws funders from both the Thai and multi-national business community.

"The company that agrees to sponsor a particular village will sit down and listen to them," says Mechai. They are not to tell the villagers what to do, but rather to offer assistance where asked. "We have a simple rule: any grant that a company gives to a village can be no more than $100 per capita over a six year period. It can be given in any amount and at any time but it must be earned in some way. It is not a hand-out. One way to earn it is through planting trees. When a villager plants a tree he gets a dollar. That dollar then goes into a fund that is managed by the village committee, half of which, I might add, are women."

The fund is called a Village Development Bank. Before a villager can borrow from it, she needs to have saved some of her own money.

Says Mechai: "When someone takes a loan, it is made public. And when they pay it back, it is made public again. They must have a very simple business plan. For example, if they want to raise chickens, they have to say how they are going to do it and how they will repay the loan. We take them to the market place so they can see what the chickens sell for. The problem occurs, of course, when they don't have sufficient skill to implement the ideas they come up with. So we see our role as helping them learn. When they borrow from the loan fund, they are charged 1% per month. The rate of repayment is 91%." The villagers in charge of the bank administer the loans.

VDP encourages both young and old to participate. A council of elders serves as the source of experience and knowledge, while a Youth Government responds to issues pertaining to young people. Many in the Youth Government go on to run for local elections. "They are a different type of leader," says Mechai referring to these young politicians. "They propose programs for the youth, for the elderly, for the handicapped. They have a program to assimilate and help those with HIV. All this they learned from their involvement in the Village Development Partnership. We need these kinds of leaders for the future of Thailand."

Mechai and his team have devoted the last forty years to the eradication of poverty in Thailand. Now he also concentrates on transforming society so that its members become more philanthropic.

People should feel the joy of helping one another and taking responsibility for the future, he says. This, he believes, is the secret to true long term sustainability.

Part of Mechai's mission in launching the Pattana schools was to introduce his idea of a *New Philanthropy* to the youngest in Thai society regardless of economic circumstances. "While sustainability of organizations like ours is key, we must build the capacity in our society for philanthropists. This is critical to our future," he says. "Every child who gets a scholarship must do community service. It is repayment to society for the opportunity they have been given." Some tutor children at a nearby government-run school, others look after the elderly and orphans.

Before the opening ceremony of the secondary school begins, Mechai makes one more stop. He follows a path towards a cream brick building, his PDA entourage still in tow. This is the Pattana Primary School, the first school he established. It is in session today and he wants to see how things are going.

Inside the large, airy hallway the student traffic flows easily. The sound of sweet and excited voices fills the air. Mechai leans into one of the classrooms. It is large, bright and has more than four sides. There is no front to the room so that the class can be taught from any vantage point. The students have a say in their curriculum. They have already decided they want to learn about Asia. They also want to study wars, and they want to have fun while they learn.

"They have just come up with the name for the course," says the teacher when she spies Mechai at the door. "It is: *Have fun with the war in Asia.*"

Outside the classroom other students are working on computers. "The principal of the primary school says we are not imparting knowledge, we are teaching the students how to get knowledge on their own," Mechai says. "With the internet they now have access to the world."

Today that same principal is running a training program for sixty teachers who have come from all over Thailand. The Ministry of Education has already determined that the Pattana School should serve as a model for others. The transformation is beginning.

Back in one of the new bamboo buildings, chairs have been arranged theater style for the opening ceremony. As Mechai takes to the podium, he pauses to scan the audience. Parents, teachers, school administrators, local government officials and members of his team await his remarks. Behind them the first incoming class of students stands shoulder to shoulder. They watch as Mechai takes a breath and begins.

"The opportunity for us to give exists, but it has not been happening enough," he says. "We must teach our children to study hard, but more importantly we must help them to be good people. If we are able to generate more good people, Thailand will be elevated to a higher level. If we want to be successful, everyone must get involved in what is happening here. This school is going to be for students to find answers in the world for themselves, not for the teachers to do it for them. And we will be a pilot for others. It will be a never-ending experiment. In addition to the children's schooling, we will elevate other aspects of their lives. We have been working with local government."

Mechai glances at a man seated next to the Head of the Department of Education, and then continues. "The school is to become a center for rural economic development, environment, social, economic, and human rights. Every one of us needs to pitch in. We are lucky that we can come to school for free, so it is our responsibility to help others less fortunate, to have a better life."

Mechai says that helping others is an opportunity, not an obligation. Those wishing to take advantage of this opportunity should find their own way to do it. For some it is simply making a donation; for others it is full involvement in funding a rural start-up, creating a school, starting a business with a social purpose, becoming a tutor to school children, caring for the sick and elderly, or adopting an orphan.

The world that Mechai envisions is one where people feel joy in creating public good; where members in society are engaged and committed to helping others and creating opportunity together; where people are no longer dependent on governments and large institutions to solve their problems. He knows that the solutions uncovered by such a culture will have a much higher probability of success and sustainability as they address not only shared needs, but also create shared outcomes. ✽

Bangkok, Thailand _____

The first time I met Mechai Viravaidya he was about to lead a group of our International Forum participants into the streets of Soi Cowboy, one of Bangkok's red light districts. It was 1997, and the AIDS crisis was in full force. If our participants were shocked that they were being put to work handing out condoms to prostitutes and their patrons, they didn't say so. But none has ever forgotten it.

It was more than a decade before I would see him again. This time we agreed to meet at his restaurant, Cabbages & Condoms, a cozy place in downtown Bangkok that serves tourists as well as locals. When I arrived, the restaurant was empty except for a man washing the floors. I passed a tall mannequin by the front door dressed as Superman in an outfit made from a rainbow of rubbers. A sign by the cash register said, "*Sorry we have no mints, please take a condom instead.*" Sure enough, beneath it was a container filled with prophylactics.

I waited for Mechai in the Captain Condom Bar, a softly lit room filled with sweet warm air from the lush gardens outside. The hanging ceiling lights were made with—what else—a variety of colored condoms. On the wall at the end of the neatly arranged bar were photographs of Mechai and people he had met or knew well.

There were family photos, too. Both Mechai's wife and daughter are involved with PDA. His daughter oversees Birds and Bees, a resort they own in Pattaya, southeast of Bangkok on the Gulf of Thailand. The profits from this enterprise help fund PDA's projects.

Mechai arrived a few minutes later. Before we sat down, he was already talking about a new idea he was working on—a public company that people could invest in, but from which they would get no return.

"Why would anyone invest in that?" I asked.

"Instead of putting your money in charity, take that money and invest in a company whose profits go towards charity," he said. In other words, watch the money you invest grow through business activities and know that the result is being reinvested in grassroots projects focused on healthcare, environment sustainability, rural schools or eradicating poverty. *How smart*, I thought. Two disciplines (business and development) that in most parts of the world operate quite independently would, as with other Mechai-inspired projects, be joined to tackle major social issues.

Mechai helped me to understand why creating financial sustainability and economic independence is so important for efforts like his—and for efforts like Nancy's, Devi's, Jockin's and Lily's for that matter. It is impossible to count on the continued support of donors. A donor's goals may change over time or they may get new pet projects and redirect funds elsewhere without much notice.

As Jockin had previously explained to me, donors also have their own agendas. They may coincide with the grassroots effort they are funding, but there may also be subtle differences. The danger is that the grassroots organization starts to "chase the money" and modifies what it is doing to appease the donors instead of doing what is the right thing given the circumstances and people involved.

In order to maintain financial independence and sustainability, Mechai funds what he does three different ways. He graciously accepts the generosity of donations and grants, but he also looks for opportunities to recover costs wherever possible. In many cases, people are willing to pay for the benefit they are receiving (such as the availability of birth control pills in rural areas). In other cases, they are willing to work to pay for something they value (such as growing vegetables to sell and help finance their children's education). Finally, profits from businesses like Cabbages and Condoms or Birds and Bees can fund projects with a social purpose. These are separate legal entities that are run like corporations, pay taxes, and have professional management. The only difference between them and regular for-profit companies is that their earnings are invested in social and economic development initiatives instead of being distributed to shareholders.

Mechai says that business and development efforts have more in common than many think. The best NGOs and grassroots efforts are run like entrepreneurial ventures. The basic skills of listening to what customers want, creating something of value, building a team of good people, securing and allocating resources, evaluating market needs, executing a plan, managing costs and learning from mistakes are all the same.

Devi Shetty believes this, too. Narayana Health is run as a business with a social purpose. Devi employs cost recovery by charging those who can afford to pay for part of their surgeries and he accepts donations to help supplement those who cannot. He also charges full price, or cost plus margin, for those who can afford to pay.

Mechai also believes that for-profit corporations are another potential partner for NGOs. The best of these want to play a role in the societies in which they do business as well as contribute in some way to improving the livelihoods and opportunity of the people in those markets. But most don't know how to initiate the process. PDA's role for more than two decades has been as liaison, facilitator, and provider of a structured approach for businesses to work in partnership with the rural poor. Donations are fine, but what PDA really seeks is the transfer of knowledge and skills that can lead to sustainable solutions and economic empowerment of the poor.

When I asked Mechai if he was still involved in AIDS education and prevention, and if he was still handing out condoms in Soi Cowboy, he shook his head. PDA has however, started the Positive Partnership Program (PPP) to address the effects of discrimination on people with HIV. Since most who are infected are poor and have trouble finding work, PPP offers them micro credit loans to start small businesses. The loans are available to partnerships between an HIV infected person and a non-infected person, usually a family member. Tied in with the loans are health services and support groups. PDA administers the program from its different centers around Thailand. PPP has been successful in spawning many small enterprises in remote parts of Thailand, though the repayment rate on these has been somewhat lower than the Village Development Partnership loans.

Mechai's inspiration comes now from his idea of a *New Philanthropy*. He knows that in his own life he has benefited from a good education and a certain set of values which guide him. But most aren't as lucky. All of us, however, can become better people when we simply give part of ourselves to helping others. The Pattana Schools, now called the Mechai Pattana Schools, have incorporated the act of giving into a child's education. It is Mechai's intent that every child be able to feel the joy of public good. It is this that will have the most far reaching and long term impact on Thai society.

For his own grandchildren he expects the same. "I want them to grow up and do whatever they want with their lives. But I want them to do something for those that are in the cold – help them, or start a business for social progress. They should always see their role as doing more for society. If they want to be in business, or start a business with a social purpose, start a foundation – I hope they will. Part of their inheritance came from land that belonged to my father which I sold. Half of it will go to the grandchildren and the other half has been given to the school. So my grandchildren will grow up and always know that a quarter of that school was started with their inheritance."

Mechai's commitment to sustainability over time took him beyond the simple financial sustainability of his work to the moral and social sustainability of his society. If every person were to be engaged in some way in helping another, fewer organizations would have to struggle to accomplish the same. It struck me after spending time with Mechai that if he was in fact successful in creating a *New*

Philanthropy movement, he would accomplish what no organization or government has: he would have empowered a nation to change itself for the better by unleashing the potential of the individual within it, not the institutions, to solve problems and take long term and personal responsibility for the outcomes. It is a powerful dream.

Halfway across the world from Mechai was another man who was wrestling with a very different set of challenges. He, too, believed in the power of a community to change itself for the better, to solve its own problems, and for individuals within it—not large institutions or government—to affect the outcome.

The Team

Distinct cultures represent unique visions of life itself,
morally inspired and inherently right. And those different
voices become part of the overall repertoire
of humanity for coping with challenges.

– WADE DAVIS

Börje Ehrstrand

When Börje Ehrstrand was offered the job as principal of Rinkeby School northwest of Stockholm, he was certain he could not turn the troubled institution around on his own. So in his negotiations with the school board he asked for three things: integration of the municipal resources for child care, social services, art, and leisure with the school resources; transfer of some of the social service budget into the school budget so he could hire necessary special needs and activity teachers; and, most importantly, authority to choose his own leadership team.

"When they offered me the position, I wanted to think about it," he says. "At the time I had a good job working with parents and students on language development at a primary school in the area, and I was making a lot of progress there."

When the school board eventually gave him what he asked for, Börje accepted the position.

The town of Rinkeby is one of over one hundred ghettos in Sweden today. It was originally developed in the 1960s as part of a government initiative to create affordable housing. Within a ten-year period, one million new or renovated low-cost dwelling places were built as part of this plan. The town's physical presence is defined by rows of closely situated, identical apartment buildings arranged around a small collection of low-lying old shops, a metro station, a library, and a school.

Though the original residents of Rinkeby were almost all ethnic Swedes or Finns, the 21st century profile is completely different. It is now a town of refugees and asylum-seekers who have come from such countries as Iraq, Iran, Somalia, Turkey, Lebanon, Korea, and the former Yugoslavia. Its inhabitants represent over sixty-five different nationalities and speak at least that many languages.

The "new" Rinkeby is the result of Sweden's liberal immigration laws and aggressive human rights stance. But poor-to non-existent integration policies have led to an unemployment rate almost three times the national average. Most of Sweden views Rinkeby as a pocket of crime, gangs, drugs, and welfare dependence; a reputation justly earned. These are bi-products of segregation and poverty but they also illuminate the friction between the many cultures that are compressed into its population of seventeen thousand. Rinkeby is a tinderbox with its roots curled around the scars left by ancient conflicts. Tensions thrive between Muslim Turks, Christian Orthodox and Albanians; Syrian Christians, Palestinians and Lebanese; Sunnis and Shiites; Serbs, Croats and Bosnian Muslims.

At the end of the 1980s, Sweden was suffering a severe economic setback. Unemployment rose, especially in towns like Rinkeby. The new immigrants were less educated than their Swedish counterparts; many did not speak the language and thus could not compete for work. Systemic unemployment bred hopelessness.

The children were the only hope for the future, but they were struggling as much as their parents. Fewer than 50% of the students at Rinkeby School were graduating. They had the lowest test scores in the country. The prejudices learned at home were being carried into the school yard, and Rinkeby School was rife with violence and vandalism. By the spring of 1989, the place was in chaos. One of the classrooms had been set on fire, most of the interior spaces had been destroyed, a third of the students had left to find an alternative school, sixteen teachers had walked out, and the leadership team had resigned their jobs. Some believed the school was beyond repair. The government was considering shutting it down. Börje Ehrstrand was its last hope.

Börje himself is an immigrant. As a young man in the 1960s, he moved from Finland to Sweden to find work. He took a teaching position in Rinkeby and stayed because housing was included in his contract. By the late 1980s, he had two decades of experience teaching younger children in the community. He knew the challenges they faced. Even so, none of the schools where he had taught had been in as terrible shape as this one.

"I saw this offer to head Rinkeby School as a real challenge and I wanted to develop myself further," he says. "I thought at the time that it might be the best job in Sweden because it could only get better. Everything had to change. There was no choice. So I took everything I had learned and recruited two people I knew I could really rely upon, and I accepted the job."

Rinkeby School offers the last two grades of compulsory education in Sweden. The simple cement buildings that make up the campus today are arranged around a large empty square. There is no sign indicating the main classroom building, nor is there a front office to check with before proceeding inside. The principal's office is one of a group of administrative rooms on the ground floor off a corridor at the back of the building. On the walls of the office are photographs of Börje shaking hands with politicians and famous people. A collection of awards has been intentionally displayed for visitors to see as soon as they enter the room.

Börje is a lean man. While genetics have played a part in this, he insists it's mainly due to the discipline of daily exercise, good sleep, and careful eating. His hair is cut short, military style. His pale cheekbones are accented by thick dark brows. In repose his expression reveals nothing of what he is thinking, but when he smiles a broad grin warms his face and softens his cold blue eyes. He is a neat and meticulous dresser; rarely without a sports coat, though he tempers it with a black turtle neck or an open collared shirt. Because he is so tall, he has to lean over and tilt his head to listen or to make eye contact with others. This makes him appear awkward and uncomfortable.

In the beginning, Börje knew that violence was the most critical problem facing the school. Until order was restored in the hallways and classrooms, students could not learn and teachers could not do their job. But the new principal also knew they all had to look beyond the chaos and envision what the school could be.

Soon after taking the job, Börje invited parents, social workers, and leaders from local mosques and churches to a meeting. He wanted to hear from all the stakeholders before determining a comprehensive plan of action. He mixed people of different backgrounds together in groups and hired translators for the many different languages spoken. He remembers the discussion that ensued and the volume of those voices. The parents took charge. They said they wanted the building to be cleaned up and repaired. They wanted the graffiti washed from the walls. They wanted to be proud of the Rinkeby School. They wanted Börje to get the money to do this.

"So I asked the government for 3 million kroner (about $350,000 U.S.) to clean up the school, and of course I got nothing," he remembers. "Then one parent told me that he knew a painter from his home country who would do it for 30,000 kroner."

After he explained that the money would be used by students, parents, and people in the community who were working together to clean up the school, Börje found a department in the Stockholm government willing to fund the effort. He couldn't require that the teachers help, but many did.

When the local painters' union complained that Börje was using children to do its work, the principal defended his decision. He explained that such work was part of the students' education, as they were developing skills for the future. By involving parents and students in the maintenance of the school, Börje did not have to spend his entire facilities budget. With the savings he hired two more teachers.

Transforming the physical space had an immediate effect on behavior. Who was going to destroy something that they themselves had helped to create?

Next Börje's team devised a process called *Immediate Action and*

Consequences to deal with bullying. If a student was violent, his parents were informed immediately and a meeting was called to determine the next steps. The troublemaker would either be placed in the *Day Care Center*—a class for troubled students—or they would be suspended and placed under their parents' supervision. In the *Day Care Center*, students attended classes in the morning and spent the afternoon in physically-demanding activities, after which most had little energy or desire to fight.

Parental commitment to the process was critical. It sent a message to the children, many of whom came from tough male-dominated homes with no tolerance for subversive behavior. As parents, teachers, and administrators united in their expectation for order and discipline, things began to change. In time the violence and bullying declined, though it never completely disappeared.

With order for the most part restored, Börje's team took on the school's curriculum. Börje strongly believed in the integration of movement and activity into the learning experience. He had seen that people learn best when they are active. He therefore encouraged teachers to take a holistic approach within the rote curriculum prescribed by the Swedish school system.

Dorothea Rosenblad was one such teacher. She was in her late forties with grown children when she first came to Rinkeby School. She had no formal teaching training, but the principal at the time needed her help. "It was not as violent when I first arrived. That happened later," Dorothea says. "But the kids were struggling and their grades were poor."

Soon after Börje arrived she was asked to join the Religious Studies Department. "When the children turned fourteen, we spent the year learning about free churches in Sweden. I remember standing in front of one class trying to explain the different views on the Eucharist between two different Christian denominations. It was ridiculous," she says.

The rules for how she could teach the subject were onerous. "I had to say '*God is said to have spoken to Moses*' instead of '*God spoke to Moses*'," she says.

The objectivity required to teach religion in this secular state drove the process to absurdity. Not only was it uninteresting, there was no connection in it for Dorothea's Muslim or non-protestant Christian students. She suspected that under the right conditions the stories in the Bible could provide a rich opportunity from which to learn, but her own secular upbringing had not prepared her for the discussions and questions that were being raised in her class. She cared enough to change that.

"Many of the children knew more about the subject than I," she says. "The Syrians, for example, had read the whole New Testament in their mother tongue by the time they came to us. And when I told the story of Genesis they corrected me saying: '*It was not Abraham who said that, it was Sarah.*' I realized then that I needed more education, so I enrolled in university to get another degree. I woke up every morning at 5:30 to study before I went to teach at school."

The stories in the Old Testament were sacred not only for the Christians, but also for Muslims and Jews. This caused Dorothea to wonder how much more these three religions had in common. "The stories captivated me. The fact that they had survived for over four thousand years was not by chance. They were filled with love, hatred, murder and betrayal," she says. "Each had a lesson from which to learn."

Dorothea saw that every child in her class—whether Muslim, Christian, Syrian, Somalian, Iraqi or Serbian—had learned the story of Abraham. In a community ravaged by conflict, there must be a way to build something positive on that.

Says Dorothea: "One morning I was watching T.V. at home. The camera was focused on a little brown boy in the mud somewhere in Asia who opened a tap and for the first time water spewed from it. And suddenly I had a revelation, something said to me: *dig where you are*. And I understood at that moment that if you want to do something important for the world, you do not need to look far, you are already there—you just have to start."

Dorothea approached Börje with an idea. She believed she could help her students find common ground by teaching religious studies through active learning. She wanted to incorporate storytelling and role-playing into her class.

Börje remembers being surprised when Dorothea came to him. But he reflects now that there were many like her who had such ideas on how to improve their classes.

"We talk a lot about respecting differences in our societies," he said. "But I was not interested in our differences. I wanted to find what we all had in common here in Rinkeby. I wanted the students to come together and support each other, not fight like people have been doing throughout history. We could not develop a future this way."

He saw the opportunity in Dorothea's idea and told her he would support her. She would, however, have to give up her role teaching Religious Studies because what she was proposing was not part of the approved curriculum. She could create a special project that would complement, but not be a part of, the course. He would find the money to fund her.

Dorothea agreed and began working on an interactive learning experience. "The students knew so little at that age—and what they knew of each other was often from the prejudices of their parents. So rather than teach, we started by telling stories," she says. "What's good about stories is that even if people are at different levels—intellectually, experientially, and emotionally—in a story everyone finds meaning. Thus no-one will feel stupid or left out. I learned that it's better to tell a story rather than read it aloud. You can then keep eye contact with the students."

The most popular story was from the book of Genesis. It recounted how Abraham sent his servant to pick a wife for his son Isaac. "It has to be someone of his own people," says Dorothea. "Turkish parents in Rinkeby send their boys to Turkey during the summer term to find Turkish wives, so we talk about this tradition and how it is still alive. Poor Isaac, he is so sad because he has lost his mother, but when he meets Rebecca he finds someone he can love. This always touches us and it makes us weep together."

The stories generated discussion, and sometimes conflict. For example, everyone agreed that Abraham had two sons: Isaac and Ishmael. But in the Jewish and Christian version of the story, Ishmael disappeared after Abraham's death while the lineage continued with Isaac. In the Muslim tradition, Ishmael, who was the eldest son, is in the Koran. Furthermore, one of his descendants was the prophet Mohammed.

"So when we tell this story it is not long before we deal with the first conflict. I warn the students that this is coming. '*Which is the favored son? Isaac or Ishmael?*' the students ask. And I say 'for you Muslims it is Ishmael, for you Christians it is Isaac. But who really knows? Only God knows.' There is no answer, but the students love the conflict and they brighten at the discussion."

As the students became more active and engaged in class they took matters into their own hands. Dorothea says: "I remember a boy from Iraq once said to me '*listen, let me take over.*' The children wanted to act out one of the stories: Abraham had hidden Sarah in a box in order to take her over the border between Palestine and Egypt. But she is discovered and taken to Pharaoh. Then comes a marvelous scene where Pharaoh tries to seduce her. So this boy took over my class and went into the crowd and told the other students what to do and he did a wonderful job. I let him do it."

Through Dorothea's class the students found common ground, just as she and Börje had hoped. They retold the old stories, discussed what the characters had done and whether their choices had been right or wrong. The moral dilemmas forced them to reflect. Eventually they realized that regardless of religion, they all faced similar choices in life.

In time, Dorothea aptly named her project after what they all had in common. Regardless of interpretation, they were all *The Children of Abraham*.

"A school does not exist in isolation," says Börje. "It is a part of a community and can influence what happens in that community. Dorothea's project was important in this way. Where I come from in Finland, the school was always the center of the village. The church was important, but the school was more important. It was always open for us; we could use it for meetings. We knew where to find the key and go in. What happened there set the tone for everything that happened in our village. I took that concept and placed it here." Rinkeby School is now open 365 days a year, and the community uses the facilities when classes are not in session. Groups and associations meet here, and young people in town use the sports and recreation complex. The idea that a school is part of the greater community fuels Börje's belief that the education of children is a holistic process. This process should not only include school work, but also the development of social competence and physical and mental wellbeing.

One of the teachers decided to mix his class on history and geography with physical activity. After having his students run fifteen to twenty minutes a day, he tracked how far they got on a map of Denmark. As the class "ran" its way across the country, students read and learned about the history and geography of each town and city they passed.

"When they were done with Denmark, they ran through Italy. When they got to Rome, they still had time in the school year. So they ran to Istanbul," says Börje. "The teacher never asked for permission to do this. He knew if he had a good idea I would have no problem with it. I found out about it because he asked me to come and help him."

Börje says it is important that teachers have a variety of experiences in their lives in addition to teaching qualifications. George Varney, an Australian musician who was working in Stockholm in the late 1980s, remembers being approached by Börje. With resources from the town's culture budget, the principal offered George an opportunity to build a new music school in Rinkeby. "He saw it as a part of a larger plan for sharing culture, education, and community activities. His idea was to integrate the school with the community," says George.

It wasn't easy. "Some students didn't find music interesting at all; others did but were forbidden by their fathers to play," says George. "A few had talent, but even those who were eager to learn had their challenges. Once a father stormed into the school demanding to know who had allowed his daughter to play without his permission. The instruments had to be kept at school so they would not be lost or bashed up in a house that did not respect them. I don't think they allowed things for their children that they themselves did not understand."

George remembers that the students who did well in music also did well in school and that over the years music became an integral part of the learning experience for them as well as the community at large. Today an annual festival provides an opportunity for the students to play music and perform for an audience that comes from Rinkeby and beyond. The festival has expanded to include short filmmaking, performance, and dance and is tied to a larger program that includes schools from Stockholm.

Rinkeby School can now choose which teachers it wants to hire. There was a time when no one wanted to work here, but today there is a waiting list. Börje laughs as he provides a candidate description that is only half in jest. "A tour guide who has had to get forty drunken Swedes onto a bus or an airplane would have the type of skills we need here."

While the quality of teachers was an important part of Börje's plan, cooperation with constituents in the broader society was just as critical. Börje engaged not only parents and social workers in school matters, but also local law enforcement, religious leaders, alumni, universities, and local businesses.

Over one hundred companies have now been involved in some way with Rinkeby School either by coming to speak with students about their career options, offering site visits, or providing internships. Students from local universities have been invited to mentor many of the Rinkeby students in engineering and sciences.

"It's important to get stimulation from people in other parts of society," says Börje. "Often we'll see new ideas that way. If we like one and want to try it out, we look for a person to develop it further and help them make it happen."

The Sports Complex on the school campus was one such idea. It received the architect prize of the year in Sweden for its design and because it involved the collaboration of the student council, community youth council, and parents in its development. The head of the student council came up with the idea for the complex in response to student frustration that there was no place to go and play games. The youth council, made up of young adults from the community, also got involved.

The project took much longer to complete than anyone expected. But in the process the students learned patience and persistence. The facility is used now by the school and also by young people in the community up to twenty-four years of age.

Rinkeby Academy is another initiative started in cooperation with the school. It was formed by older alumni who had become professionals, doctors, dentists, and business leaders. The Academy helps current students chart a professional path and then to find work.

By 2007, almost twenty years after Börje became principal, the school had been almost entirely rebuilt, matriculation rates were approaching 97%, and a number of the students had scored 100% on the national exams. Of the more than 500 pupils, one-fifth came from other districts because the school had developed such a good reputation for preparing students.

"Many said that these children would have no future after school except for prison. But our students surprised us all," says Börje. "They have succeeded in their lives. Of course, we were not successful with every single one; some do get in trouble and go to prison. But it gives one a lot of energy to work here because you do see the improvement."

Turnover in the town of Rinkeby used to be high, as people left in search of better schools for their children. As the situation at the school stabilized and academic performance improved, families stayed.

In time parents' expectations changed as well. In the beginning the concern was simply about getting the situation under control. "Then the parents became more interested in their own child's progress and test results rather than the betterment of the school," says Börje. "It is not the same fighting spirit it was back then. But then we don't need it in the same way now. Today our challenge is how to help new students in Rinkeby to develop their language skills and the tools they will need to learn and communicate and be prepared for a Europe without borders."

Though the situation has improved dramatically, Rinkeby School has its problems. In 2008, parents began speaking out on the inequities at the school; some students, particularly good ones, were given preferential treatment and access to better resources, they said. They also complained that Börje was spending too much time talking to the press and politicians about his success and less time on the daily operations of the school. This was true. Börje was proud of what they had accomplished and more than willing to make speeches and accept awards for it.

Reflecting on his tenure, Börje says, "Finding solutions has been the most interesting part of this job. It's not as complicated as one might think. Changing the way things have been done can look complicated at the beginning, but if you take it step by step, it is much easier."

He concedes that he is surprised how often good ideas have been turned down. He never expected to hear so many people say "no," whether in government, social services or in other organizations set up to help the children. One would think it should be rather simple to do the right thing, but it doesn't appear to happen that way when many agendas are involved. For example, when Börje realized that the school was paying exorbitant taxi fares to send disabled children to special schools in downtown Stockholm every day, he made a case for those students to attend Rinkeby School.

"The key to a successful future for these children is that they need to be integrated into the school system early. They are from families around here and have played in the same playgrounds. The other children here don't see them as different. So don't create problems where there are no problems," says Börje.

At first those with the authority to make these changes resisted. Then Börje noted that one single student's annual taxi fees to downtown Stockholm was more than it would cost to employ a dedicated teacher. "When I explained it this way to the politicians, they became very interested. Now we have thirty to forty disabled students in two schools in Rinkeby."

Börje insists that it was his team and all the other stakeholders that helped turn around Rinkeby School. "During an effort like this, you get help from more people than you think you will at the beginning. Why is that? I don't know. But it happens." ❁

Rinkeby, Sweden ―――――――――――――――――――――――

The Nordic sun cast a flat light across the neatly swept streets of Rinkeby. Pale patches of green grass hinted of the approaching spring. It had been more than ten years since I'd seen Börje Ehrstrand. He was close to retirement, a state he was reluctant to embrace. The job of principal had been passed to a capable young woman. She had already built upon Börje's legacy. The energy level in the school was higher than during my previous visit; the students I encountered were more confident and articulate.

Börje didn't look any older than the last time we had met. He was still as physically active as he had always been, diligent about his health and passionate about his life's work. After we met in his office, which was also unchanged, he walked with me through the quiet hallways of the school and out a side door. We stood together at the edge of the school property for a while observing the town in front of us. People were going about their business. Women in colorful headscarves and long thick dresses covered in layers of wool pushed baby strollers in pairs. Dark-haired young men passed without a glance. An old man with a curling moustache sat on a bench and observed the routine around him with mild curiosity.

After a few minutes I asked Börje what he had learned from his years in Rinkeby that might help a Europe now struggling with the integration of its immigrants.

"It is important not to see it as a problem," he said. "It is important to find the possibilities in it. The newcomers have a drive to succeed and to make things better. Don't turn them away. Educate them, integrate them, and allow them to contribute to making this society richer."

Like Mechai, Börje is a tenacious leader who believes education is a country's hope for the future. But unlike the Thai who built a school where none existed, Börje inherited a broken legacy. His financial resources came not from donations or businesses with a social purpose, as Mechai's had, but rather from his own creative and careful management of pre-set budgets funded by taxpayer dollars.

I told Börje about what Mechai had done with his Pattana schools and repeated what the Thai had once said to me: *when you are endowed with cash, you stop thinking up new ideas. But when you don't have enough money, you are always thinking about how to get resources and how to use what you've got to do things differently.*

"Would you agree?" I asked.

He nodded. "It is the same way here. We did not have enough money to do what we wanted to, so I had to listen to the people around us. They figured out the solutions to the problems."

Dorothea Rosenblad and George Varney helped me to better

understand the different roles that many people play in bringing about a change of this magnitude. While Börje was the public face for the school and became famous for what happened, he was the ringleader for the bigger show. He got the process going by helping to stabilize the situation. With the threat of violence under control, the school community began to heal. And as Lily Yeh demonstrated in North Philadelphia and other places around the world, once people heal they are better prepared to rebuild.

Börje was able to engage those who had the most to gain from changing the school—parents, students, teachers and community members. He helped them find common ground, just as Jockin had in his community. Next he created the space for them to innovate by keeping at bay the bureaucrats, rule makers and gate keepers. He secured resources to support the stakeholders' ideas, and he empowered them to transform the educational experience.

It was this collective effort of individuals working together as a team, not one heroic leader, that transformed a school expected to fail into a community that succeeded.

I was on my way to the metro station to catch a train back to Stockholm when I ran into Dorothea Rosenblad. She was heading towards the town library and asked if I'd like to join her. The library, she explained, is the heart of the community. It also happened to house Dorothea's personal collection of books and artifacts from the three world religions whose roots can be traced to the story of Abraham. The library's biggest draw, however, were the display cases in which Dorothea and her students had arranged small handmade figures of Abraham, Joseph, Rebecca, Angel Gabriel, Jesus, Mary, John the Baptist and Elizabeth in scenes from the Bible, the Koran and the Torah. The stories were recounted through recordings played through headphones provided by the library. They had also been written on cloth, translated by students into the many languages of Rinkeby.

"I was here one day when a lady all dressed in black, fully covered, and wearing gloves came in," said Dorothea. "She went to look at the crib with Jesus in it and then read the part that tells the story from the Bible. Then she turned and read the part of the story told in the Koran and then returned to the version from the Bible. And then she turned and left."

Dorothea believes that through the *Children of Abraham*, the teenagers were able to unlearn some of the prejudices they had been taught at home and begin to identify with each other. But it was in that moment, as she watched the woman in black, that she realized what she and the children were doing had spread beyond the school and was affecting the community.

"Empathy enables us to identify with others," she said. "One has to dehumanize people if one is going to send someone out to fight. But if you look someone in the eye and understand their story, it is hard not to see them as a human being."

"Has what you've done made a difference?" I asked.

"You can only hope that it has changed minds towards a friendlier way," she said. "But I don't think you can ever prove it, because the world is not yet saved."

I thought of what she had said to me earlier: how if you want to do something important you need only *dig where you are*. For many years Dorothea had managed a family and run a busy home in a nice suburb outside of Stockholm. Then one day, an acquaintance from church asked if she would help teach at a school in an immigrant ghetto, a place Dorothea had never been and only heard about. Dorothea's children were grown and she had the time to do something new, so she took the job. She had neither formal teaching experience, nor academic credentials in the subject she eventually taught. But she overcame that. Through trial and error and incorporating ideas from others including her students, she ended up making a meaningful difference for a group of children, their families and a community. This was also the case with Lily. She was an artist, mother, teacher and wife who during one summer holiday accepted a small art project in North Philadelphia. It was much the same way for Nancy, Devi, Mechai and Jockin—who each started a small thing that ultimately became a movement that transformed people's lives. In the beginning each had simply dug where they were.

Dorothea is still teaching the Children of Abraham but it is now part of a curriculum offered by an organization she has created called Abraham's Barn. She develops interactive learning and storytelling experiences for children and adults in Rinkeby as well as others across Sweden. Her focus continues to be on understanding what we all have in common, identifying with each other and building empathy—something that is ever more important in Europe today.

Dorothea has helped me to see that to *dig where you are* means that you believe that no single person is more worthy of your support than another—that regardless of economics, background, or circumstances, if you see a way to help another because of something you know how to do, then that is enough. We cannot predict where or when the opportunity will arise and quite often it looks nothing like what we think it should. But if you pay attention and listen, you will see opportunities all around you.

Almost a month to the day after my last visit to Rinkeby a gang of twenty-year-olds were stopped trying to gate-crash a student dance. The gang retaliated by throwing bricks into buildings and raised chaos in the streets. After two days of rioting, they had left a stain of destruction and had set fire to a neighborhood bank. Then they burned Rinkeby Academy, the small building next to the school, to the ground. The police and fire workers tried to restore order. In the ensuing struggle, the rioters managed to deface the local police station too.

I thought of the team at Rinkeby School when I heard the news. I recalled how proud Börje had been when he recounted how graduates had built Rinkeby Academy to help current students. I wondered if the rioters had been former students. When interviewed by the press, a local resident said he felt that the crowd had been acting out in frustration and rage over their circumstances in life.

I realized then that the challenges that this community faces may never be gone. Just as the problems that face the slum dwellers, the Tibetan villagers, and the residents in North Philadelphia may never be completely resolved. There will always be something that causes suffering.

There is no doubt that Rinkeby today is a stronger community than it was before because of what it went through to heal and re-build its school. The question is not whether it has found the right solution to its problems, but whether the people who live there have the tools and resilience to continually confront challenges, work together to overcome them, and then move forward.

In San Francisco there is a woman who more than anyone, knows that we cannot control what has yet to happen. For more than half her life she has lived among convicted criminals and drug addicts where working together has been the only way to move forward.

The Inmate

Our deepest fear is not that we are inadequate.
Our deepest fear is that we are powerful beyond measure.

– MARIANNE WILLIAMSON

Mimi Silbert

"There isn't a person around who feels a damn thing for a third generation gang member," says Mimi Silbert. "Nobody happens to like them. But I happen to love them."

Mimi is barely five feet tall, yet has the presence of a man twice her size. When she enters a room, everyone knows it. Though she is well into her seventies, she could pass for twenty years younger. Her eyes are bright blue, like semiprecious aquamarine; and they move quickly, missing nothing. Her thick brown mane of hair hangs loosely around her shoulders. She has never bothered to style it or cut it short the way another women her age might have. Those types of personal details don't interest her.

On the table in front of her is a lunch of hash browns, eggs, hollandaise sauce and Velveeta cheese. At her feet lies Maple the dog, a fluffy brown bundle of fur that looks more like a teddy bear than a canine. She watches as a young man in a shirt and tie approaches with a plate of vegetables.

"Put it here, Romero," says Mimi gesturing to a spot near the corner of the room.

Romero chuckles as he bends his massive six-foot frame to set the dog's lunch carefully on the tile floor.

The smell of sautéed vegetables and baked apple-cinnamon wafts into the private dining room while the bustling lunchtime crowd gains momentum in the main space outside. Today's specials at the Delancey Street Restaurant include roasted garlic chicken and crab cakes served with rice and mango papaya salsa. The menu combines old recipes from Mimi's childhood in an immigrant neighborhood outside Boston, with recent concoctions created by Delancey Street residents.

There are about four hundred people living in the larger complex adjoining this restaurant on San Francisco's busy waterfront. Ninety percent are men. They are a cross section of society: white, black, Latino, tall, short, fat, thin. But they differ from their fellow citizens in one important regard. Most have come after serving multiple prison terms for violent crimes. The average number of felony convictions per resident is eighteen. A few are here after hitting rock bottom as junkies, living on the street and selling anything they can for money to buy drugs.

In spite of the profile of its inhabitants, however, Delancey Street does not employ a single guard or social worker, warden or counselor to keep things in line. The place is run entirely by its residents. There is only one among them who is neither drug addict nor criminal, and that is the tiny septuagenarian putting Velveeta on her hash browns.

Mimi calls Delancey Street a *Residential Learning Community.*

Others who know about its success call it a world-class solution to criminal rehabilitation. The statistics bear this out: 85-90% of those who make it through here *never* return to prison. Rather, they go on to lead meaningful lives as contributing members of society. As the recidivism rate in the U.S today is 70-80%, the success of this place is something many have tried to understand.

Before developing Delancey Street, Mimi was a professor at University of California-Berkeley, an expert in criminology and psychology with two PhDs. In 1971 she left her career to assist John Maher, a recovered drug addict and ex-con, in setting up a unique self-supporting rehabilitation center. Convicts and addicts would live together, get off drugs, finish high school, learn a skill or trade, and develop the self-esteem needed to live as productive members of society. Maher was convinced that this model would be more effective and sustainable than traditional rehab programs that incorporated outside experts to implement solutions created elsewhere.

Mimi was the mother of young twin boys at the time, and in addition to teaching at Berkeley, she was a consultant to police departments, prison systems and halfway houses. She had seen and experienced enough by then to be discouraged by the ineffectiveness of programs for convicts and addicts. Maher's idea, however, intrigued her.

With only $1,000, the unlikely pair launched their effort for a handful of recovering addicts in a one-bedroom apartment. Within two years they had grown to one hundred residents and had purchased a run-down and neglected mansion, once the Russian Consulate in Pacific Heights. Though the neighbors objected when they moved in, the residents in the old Russian Consulate won them over by renovating the mansion and patrolling the neighborhood to keep criminals away. By 1984, there were over three hundred and fifty residents living together, behaving like a family and looking out for each other and the neighborhood.

The results of what they were doing were impressive and were making the case for a powerful alternative to prison and traditional drug rehabilitation programs. But all was not well. In 1985, John Maher returned to drugs and alcohol thereby breaking one of the cardinal rules agreed to by all residents who entered the place. The residents and extended family tried to help him, but to no avail. After crashing his car and endangering others, he was asked to leave Delancey Street. The rules established back then, still apply and they apply to all residents – including the founders. Maher died three years later.

With Maher gone, Mimi had to run Delancey Street on her own. After struggling with the city government and zoning authorities, she secured a long-term lease on the site where the current building stands at 600 Embarcadero. With no qualifications or experience, she then designed the complex and managed its construction and financing. With an eleventh hour loan from Bank of America for $10 million, she and the residents were able to complete the Delancey Street triangle which today houses one hundred and seventy apartments for up to five hundred residents, a theatre, auditorium, dining hall, restaurant, retail locations, and meeting rooms. They repaid the loan in three and a half years with revenues generated from a number of small businesses they created and ran.

The project was one of the greatest challenges they faced as a community. That the residents and Mimi were neither qualified nor had the skills to build and finance such an undertaking didn't stop them. They learned as they went, even when it meant taking down and rebuilding the same walls seven times because they were crooked.

"This population has been passive for so long and has no self-esteem. And you can't give self-esteem to someone," says Mimi. "Self-esteem comes from doing things, from taking a chance, putting yourself out there and making something happen."

Mimi has had years to build her self-esteem, but she acknowledges that she started from a better place than most of the residents at Delancey Street. "I was brought up by people who were very loving. They didn't like money much—which was probably good. It made it easier for me to follow my gut, not the money. And I have always had a pretty strong gut."

For over forty years Mimi's gut has told her the same thing: *If a person wants to get better they have to start by helping someone else.*

Delancey Street Restaurant is one of a number of businesses that the residents run. It is a popular spot in San Francisco for good food at a good price. It is no secret that the chefs, bus boys, and waiters have rap sheets longer than the list of entrees. This fact is printed on the menu for everyone to see.

In the United States today, there are approximately 2.3 million incarcerated men and women. Only about 200,000 are in Federal prisons, while the majority are split fairly evenly between local jails and state prisons. In California the local jail population is close to 80,000. It is from this group that most of Delancey Street's residents are drawn. A candidate who is awaiting sentencing may approach Delancey Street and ask to be considered for a spot in lieu of serving time in prison. If pre-selected he will be interviewed by several residents. He will be asked to talk about his life, what he has done and why he wants to come to Delancey Street. He will almost always lie and the residents know this. Through the interviews, enough will be learned to decide whether to invite him in. Once accepted, he will be given a letter to take to the judge at sentencing.

Romero, who is now the Maître D' of Delancey Street Restaurant, came five years ago from jail. "I was in juvenile hall when I was fifteen," he says. "When I turned eighteen, I was sent to jail. I wanted to go. It was what I thought I was going to do with my life. I had friends in prison and an older cousin, who I looked up to, who was doing a life sentence."

After five separate trips to prison, Romero was arrested again. He had heard of Delancey Street as an alternative to serving time. Years earlier he had interviewed for a spot. He had been accepted, but decided against going. He wasn't ready then to leave the people and life that he knew. This time, however, he was facing a twelve year sentence. He wondered if there was an alternative. When Delancey Street approached him again, he was ready to come.

Romero grew up in a community north of San Francisco. His parents were alcoholics who fought constantly and played no role in raising him. He had an aunt who might have been a better influence, but she lived over an hour away. Neighborhood gangs offered a sense of family that Romero couldn't find at home. They congregated in the park behind his house. His cousin already a member, always had a new weapon he wanted to show off.

Says Romero: "I just wanted to be accepted. By the time I was sixteen, I had done a number of shootings and stabbings and nothing went through my mind like I shouldn't do this. You know I never had any kind of thoughts like that. I said, 'I'll do it.' I was just lonely and angry growing up."

His dark eyes don't soften when he smiles. It is as if he is practicing facial expressions and hasn't got all the pieces to work together yet. Still, were one to meet him on the street, he would appear as just another college student or young professional, not a convicted criminal with multiple felonies.

"You didn't laugh once in the first two years," Mimi says to Romero. Having finished her lunch, she motions for Romero to take a seat at the table next to her. "No one had ever seen you smile. You were just this tight ice cube violent thing."

Romero nods. "Until the Elf Dinner," he says.

"Yes, when you and everyone else walked behind me into the room shooting your legs up in the air singing *Here comes Santa Claus.*" Mimi starts singing the popular holiday song. After a minute Romero joins in. Maple stirs on the floor, catching Mimi's attention. "Sorry baby," Mimi says in a squeaky voice reserved for puppies. "We didn't mean to wake you."

Romero remembers that Mimi made him eat everything put in front of him at the Elf Dinner that year. He ate until, as he says, he was "food drunk." Then he started to giggle. Then the giggle turned into a laugh. Then he couldn't stop laughing.

"Then someone said: 'That's Romero!!! He's laughing!'" Mimi says, her voice rising in excitement.

"Yeah. I kept looking at you and I couldn't stop laughing," says Romero.

"Sometimes it's just about eating and laughing and forgetting who you are," Mimi says. "And realizing you are a part of a community that is laughing at themselves. All of a sudden you break through; something happens and you look around and say *I like all these people.*"

"These are my people," Romero says softly.

"When we started this place, we had first generation gangsters," Mimi says. You used to be able to reach them by saying things like: *Your mother left wherever and crawled across the country and cleaned toilets so that you could become a fucking junkie and not give a shit about her, get seven people pregnant.* But that's not true now. Today they are third generation. They come in and their grandmothers are writing to them saying: *Get out of there, someone took revenge on your cousin and we need you to take revenge on them and we need the money from your selling dope.* This is the way they live. They have so developed an underclass reality (I have always called them an underclass) that has nothing whatsoever to do with anything else."

Mimi says that when the politicians today talk about the divide between the people in our society they have no idea what the reality is. They are referring to money—who has it and who doesn't. But that's not the problem.

"It used to be that people who came here were in despair, but they knew what hope was. Now they don't even know what hope is. This is what they have been born into and what everyone else they know has been born into. At some point, however, some don't want to go to prison for the rest of their lives. So they come here, but they have no idea what's possible; and I don't mean they have no idea that they might someday go to a museum and learn about art. I mean that they don't understand that there will be a day when they won't want to kill everybody that's not in their gang," she says.

After they've been here for a while, after they've experienced what it's like to do a job and complete it or do something for someone else, things start to change.

Romero has hope now. He never cooked before coming here. He hadn't even boiled an egg. Now he bakes breads and makes desserts. He says it makes him feel good to cook for people. In the beginning fellow residents taught him to be a bus boy. Then he graduated to pastry chef. Eventually he was promoted to the job he has now.

The average stay for a resident here is four years. "When I first got here I thought – do I stay? Do I want to do this?" Romero says. "I was so into gang life that I knew if I stayed here too long I wouldn't be accepted back and then I can't go anywhere. That was my biggest battle. I didn't do much of anything. I just worked. I put my head down and just worked. It took me awhile; it took me a couple of years."

"You have to stay here at least two years. That's what the courts feel is right," Mimi says. "But you'll know when you're done and that's when you leave." She smiles. "We do everything the opposite of prison. That's why you ring the bell to get in that front door. And it's open whenever you want to go out."

Romero knows this. So what keeps him here?

In the over forty years Delancey Street has been in existence, only a small number of residents have left before they were ready. "But then a lot have come back," says Mimi. "They went back to their parole officers or their girlfriends and said *are you kidding me?* and then they came back."

They realize that they have changed, that their lives have changed and that they don't want anything to do with who and how they used to live.

"But I don't take everyone back who decides to leave early because I want to be known as a place that's hard to get into. There are always a few who only make it three days, or a day. They either don't like it, or don't like the work."

But for the rest, like Romero, there is something that keeps them here—whether it's seeing others every day who are making it work, whether it's because they feel connected to the group with whom they have to spend every waking hour, whether it's because they like the food or the work, or because they have no other choice. Everyone has a reason.

Residents are assigned apartments based on their tenure and seniority. The new residents are grouped together in one part of the complex. They sleep in rooms of eight or nine and they go everywhere together. If one is slow in the morning and makes them all late for breakfast, they all get in trouble.

The emphasis here is on education and building skills to live productive lives as members of society. Most arrive illiterate. By the time they leave, they must have either a high school diploma or passed a high school equivalency exam. They must also learn at least three marketable skills from cooking to accounting to manual labor.

What changes your life is changing what you do not what you say you're going to do, says Mimi. Traditional therapy helps you to understand what got you into trouble in the first place but it does not lead to a better life unless you act on it; and figuring out how to do that on your own is nearly impossible if you are a self-destructive personality. Residents at Delancey Street put what they learn into action every day. The term they use for that process is *"Act as if."*

If you want to be a decent human being then *Act as if* you are one again and again. Even though you don't care about anyone but yourself, because that is how you have survived until now, *Act as if* you do and eventually you will. If you want to be someone with a real job someday, then put on a coat and tie, do your work day after day and eventually you will be that person.

In 2010, Delancey Street was shaken when Mimi was diagnosed with cancer. She underwent treatment and while in recovery she suffered two minor strokes. As if that were not enough, she hit her head and suffered a concussion that caused a temporary loss of memory.

"I couldn't think of the names of a lot of people in Delancey Street. I thought, *Oh my god I've known their stories since the beginning, now what will happen?*" she says. "The first time I got up in front of the residents after my strokes I couldn't talk very well. But I laughed and made jokes anyway. Then I reminded them about our principles. One of the residents said – 'oh I thought *Act as if* meant to act as if you are busy when the older residents come along.' And I said, 'You've got it absolutely wrong. Let me explain. For example– this entire speech I am giving you is one big *Act as if*. Really I'd rather be in my bed with my box of white chocolates crying. But that won't help me; it won't help you and won't help the world. So even though this is the worst time for me and I feel horrible I am going to *Act as if* I love my life'."

Today Mimi is back in almost full force. She tends to tire more easily at the end of the day and still forgets a few things—but then so do most people ten years younger than she.

From the sidewalk, the Delancey Street complex looks like luxury condominiums. The buildings are arranged around an immaculate courtyard behind a wrought iron gated entrance. The second and third floors are exclusively apartments, while the street level units are, for the most part, occupied by small businesses run by residents—an artist's framing studio, an auto body shop, dog grooming, a print shop, and a cafe/bookstore.

The first business, a moving company, was created while still in Pacific Heights. Mimi got the idea when she watched a couple of residents help lift a neighbor's grand piano. "If there was one thing that prison gives you, it's big muscles," she says. Delancey Street Movers has grown to become the largest moving company in Northern California.

Today the portfolio of enterprises also includes catering, furniture design, Christmas tree sales, transportations services for the elderly and people with disabilities, construction, marketing incentives, and a credit union.

In the center of the complex is a small pool, a community events room and a movie screening theatre which is also available for rent to outsiders. In one of the buildings is the kitchen and dining room, the Club Room for gatherings, and the Vatican Room where the more tenured residents meet to discuss the social wellbeing of their community.

Delancey Street is a private nonprofit organization. It receives no government funding. Seventy percent of its operating expenses are covered by the revenues from its many businesses. The remaining 30% of revenues come from private donations or donations in-kind.

Residents are responsible for running the daily operations of

Delancey Street as well as training and teaching each other. A convicted thief manages the financial records. The irony is not lost on him when he explains that his daily duties now entail being trusted to manage money that is not his. Many who have had this job before him have gone on to professions in bookkeeping, accounting, and business management. The moving company is run by another convicted thief, who points out that today he is still taking things from homes; only now he is hired by the owner and is even paid to do so.

The complex is kept clean by the newer residents who sweep and mop the stone tiles daily. When you first get here, you are assigned the dirty jobs; and you do them all day long. When you get good enough at sweeping and mopping, you are promoted to another job—but not before you teach what you've learned to someone else.

"We keep them busy so they don't have time to think about how much they hate each other or how hard it is here," explains the Head of Maintenance, who himself arrived at Delancey Street a couple of years ago.

There are two rules by which everyone must abide: no violence or threat of violence, and no drugs or alcohol. If you break either, you are out. You go back to prison if you're a convicted criminal and back to the streets if you're an addict.

There has been no violence at Delancey Street since it was founded, but there is a lot of anger: anger at society, anger at family members, anger at rival gangs, and anger at themselves. But anger is not necessarily bad. As Romero says about the candidates he interviews: "I look for a little anger in a person because it tells me he has energy, something that drives him, and so he'll probably do well here. A meek or quiet person won't do as well. But there can be too much anger. Sometimes we're wrong about people."

On more than one occasion, Mimi has questioned some of the decisions regarding new recruits. But she concedes that on the whole the residents are smarter at picking candidates than she. They know all the games and lies, she explains.

"Every day we go to jails to interview people who are waiting to go to prison," she says. "I tell the residents to take ten people, and they pick the ten worst people they can find. I like to say we are just like Harvard. Except Harvard goes out of their way to pick the top 1% and we go out of our way to find the bottom 1%."

Mimi says that in spite of the changes on the outside over the past four decades, Delancey Street has not changed how it does things on the inside. Experts and consultants have suggested that as a world-class organization, it should expand what it is doing, replicate it, roll it out and scale it up. But Mimi will have none of it.

"I guess more people know us now than used to. But if you understand the world, you know that most of the time they raise you up so they can tear you down later," she says. "No, we're not world-class. We are the same assholes who have to keep getting it together, pooling our resources, learning decency, getting some power, and moving forward."

She has never been interested in placing a priority on expanding the scope of what she does by increasing the number of residents she takes in. Her focus is not on numbers, but in facilitating real and sustainable transformation. She has, however, created smaller versions of Delancey Street San Francisco in Los Angeles, North Carolina, Santa Fe and New York.

Every person who leaves any of these locations and makes a new life is equipped—and usually eager—to help another do the same. "That is how you create scale," Mimi says. "And it happens because when A helps B, A gets better, when B helps C, B gets better, C helps D and C gets better. Sure one person might have started something, but what really matters is that each is helping the other and making things better, and each one is teaching someone else what they have learned."

When a resident feels that they have learned everything they can from Delancey Street, they make their case in front of a council of other residents. If their case is accepted, the transition process begins. Mimi knows this process is difficult so she tells them not to worry and not to rush it.

A resident can still live at Delancey Street while they settle into a new job, make new friends, start putting things together, and finding their own place. Then naturally they start to separate, as any young family member does when they grow up and leave home. Once they keep a job for three to six months, they start what Mimi calls the "change of address" phase.

"Some who leave come back all the time for dinner. Some only come on holidays," says Mimi. "Some belong to golf clubs now and don't want anyone in the club to know they have a past, so we don't see them again."

Those who have been in the program keep in touch with each other on Facebook and through social media. Mimi is not a part of that dialogue. She is not terribly interested in technology as a medium for communication; she doesn't even have an e-mail address. Also, she believes they should be left to begin their own lives away from her. It is enough for her to know that they are still looking out for each other after they leave here.

"When someone does something for someone else they feel good about themselves, it's not when something is done for you," she says. It is the same for those still inside Delancey Street as it is for those who have moved on. When someone feels good about themselves, builds self-esteem, much more is possible.

Mimi has given a lot of thought recently to who her successor may be. But she also knows the future of Delancey Street may not turn out the way she has planned. Someday it will be out of her hands. But if even one life is changed for the better because someone does something for someone else, it will be worth it.

Whatever the future, Mimi and Delancey Street have helped to transform thousands of lives; and these transformed men and women have already gone on to help thousands more.

Everyone who passes through Delancey Street learns the secret to changing a life: *Each One Teaches One*. It's that simple and that complex. And it works. ✿

San Francisco, U.S.A.

Because of Mimi's illnesses, I was not allowed to see her for a year. I had the feeling that the residents were protecting her. Disappointed as I was, I found it reassuring that they wanted to make sure she had recovered completely before she could receive visitors. When at last she was well enough, I got a call from a resident at Delancey Street inviting me to come and visit.

It had been over a decade since I had last been to the complex. The buildings were in excellent condition, recently painted, and clean. Inside, the restaurant was as busy as ever. I heard Mimi laughing and talking even before I saw her. When she spied me her eyes lit up, she smiled, and then she hugged me. She has always made me feel as if I was the most important person in the room.

"You look the same," she said after stepping back and sizing me up.

So did she. In spite of her illness, Mimi had barely changed in twelve years. Her brown hair was still thick, with barely a streak of grey. Her soft skin made her look years younger.

She asked where I had been all this time, what I had been doing, and how my father was, as she had met him, too. I had last seen Mimi when I brought a group of business leaders to meet with her as part of an International Forum in San Francisco. The focus of this particular Forum had been on technology and innovation and how that was changing the world. Visiting a group of convicted felons was about as far away from that as one could get; and yet it had the greatest impact on our group. The business leaders were inspired by the residents and how they were changing their lives. They learned a great deal from how Mimi led her organization. In the years to come, our clients would talk about this experience wherever we met them in the world. One man even returned with his family to see her again.

It was after this experience with Mimi that we began to purposefully seek out people who were changing the world from the grassroots in order to include them in our programs. After Mimi, I found Lily, then Nancy, and then many others.

Where had I been since I'd last seen her? I told Mimi about my trips to Mumbai where I had learned about the urban poor movement from Jockin. I recounted the day I sat on straw mats with Celine and the pavement women and told them the story of Delancey Street.

Mimi liked that.

"I asked the women if they had any idea why Delancey Street worked, why when people leave they don't go back to prison," I said. "And the women didn't even hesitate. Many had family members already in jail. They said: '*Of course we know why it works. Because when you go to prison, you have everything done for you and if you have everything done for you, you never learn.'*

"I have chills hearing that," said Mimi.

"These women are illiterate and they live on the street and they get it better than anyone," I said. "They get what you've done here."

"Of course they do," Mimi said.

I told Mimi that it was after that meeting with the women in Mumbai that I knew I had to share what I was seeing, hearing and learning from the people I had met in my life. It wasn't enough that just the participants of our International Forum knew. "Six months later I left my work so I could spend time with you and others I had known who were solving big issues in small ways. I thought the stories were important to tell and many didn't have the voice or the time to tell them," I explained.

"And some of us who do have a voice, don't want to use it because we are too busy doing what we do," said Mimi. "Isn't it funny that there is something in your stomach that keeps telling you what you have to do? What's in your gut leads you to your life. The call will come at some point for all of us, but most people aren't listening when it does because they've got themselves entrapped in too many unnecessary things—shopping at Saks, shopping for an Audi. If you're not open, you can't hear what's calling you."

The others had heard the call, too. Lily had been afraid of it at first. For Devi, it had come through a conversation with Mother Teresa. Jockin saw the injustice all around him and felt compelled to gather others and fight it, Mechai and Börje found their call by seeing opportunity in the work they were already doing, as had Nancy. Each made a choice supported by their beliefs, their values, and their instincts; even while others tried to talk them out of it.

Nancy wonders still, what would have happened to millions of Tibetans had she listened to those who told her that what she wanted to do could not be accomplished; Devi keeps a framed quote on his desk to remind himself every day that "*Most of things worth doing in the world have been declared impossible before they were done.*"

"There is a revolution happening," said Mimi. "But it is so gradual that you cannot see it yet. Slowly the big shots who have been running the world are not going to have the same power anymore; only they don't realize it yet. I think it will be a very different world in the future, the kind of world where people believe, fight, and make something happen because it comes from their gut; not because they have been hired as a professional to do it."

Mimi says this revolution is not like the ones she tried to start as a student marching at Berkeley in the 1960s. Rather this one is about people making a difference by working with others, not waiting for an institution or government to do it for them. She has seen it happen already. If the bottom of the barrel in society—criminals and drug addicts—can transform themselves and each other, then anything is possible.

"People always ask me: did you have a vision?" said Mimi. "My answer is, no." The path, she believes, is revealed once you follow your gut.

Because there was no road map, no strategic plan, no precedent for creating something like Delancey Street, Mimi relied on her personal values and beliefs to guide her. From the beginning she had faith that if one person helps or teaches another, he or she will change himself or herself for the better as well. That became the platform upon which Delancey Street was built and continues to thrive.

To ensure that it continues, Delancey Street must be self-sustaining, says Mimi. Like Mechai and Devi, she does not want to be dependent on donors or government funding for survival. Such support is unreliable and often contingent upon adherence to certain restrictions and regulations—most of which are designed to protect and minimize risk, not cultivate innovation. Being self-sustaining also requires residents to take personal responsibility for the daily operations and ongoing viability of the community in which they live. This cultivates important life and work skills.

"There is something I never knew until I had children," said Mimi. "You can't make anybody do anything, no matter who you think you are. You can try to motivate them, but that's it. I remember telling my kids at a certain age that I had given them all the values and ideals I could, that from now on I would just be their backboard. '*You are going to be shooting your own baskets,*' I told them. You might think you can mold your children, but you can't. You can be there and you can be the role model, but then you have to walk away."

Her role is not much different for the third generation gang members with whom she lives now. She is helping them prepare for life, encouraging them, teaching them and connecting them with others. Then, when the time is right she will step out of their way.

Dig Where You Are

Don't believe what your eyes are telling you.
All they show is limitation.
Look with your understanding,
find out what you already know,
and you will see the way to fly.

– RICHARD BACH

Values In Common

When Dorothea Rosenblad said that if you want to do something important for the world you just have to dig where you are, I knew I had found what I had been searching for. What I had wanted to know all along was how seven people had accomplished what they had, when so many others before them had tried and failed. What could I learn from them that I could share with others?

Everyone in this book started on their path by taking one step forward. At the time they weren't really sure where they were going, what the end would look like, or that they would affect so many people. They simply encountered a situation, believed that they could help, and did something about it. Perhaps this was the secret to their success: at the onset they had no grand plans, no big dreams, and no long term goals and so they were open to where the circumstances took them. It was only when they got further into what they were doing and involved others that a path emerged.

The processes each followed were initially more intuitive than deliberate, though some became methodical and prescriptive as they gained experience and scope. In most cases each person was able to articulate afterwards how things had fallen into place, but was quick to admit that at the time they didn't know how it would come together. They acted on the ideas and input of others as well as their own values and instincts in finding the most efficient and effective course to take. The artist, the psychologist, the doctor, the teacher, the economist, the community organizer, and the surgeon are strangers to this day and yet they share so much.

There were common elements in all of their efforts, eight of which are outlined below. These do not necessarily provide a road map for solving all of our problems, but after years of traversing the world and learning from people who have made a difference, I am confident that they are values that anyone who decides to dig where they are will want to consider.

Make it Safe

Before tackling the issue that faced them, each in their own way made sure that the situation was stable and the people with whom they were working felt safe. Nowhere was this better illustrated than at Rinkeby School. Börje Ehrstrand knew there was nothing that could be done until the violence and bullying was under control. Once the alliance between teachers and parents was forged and the consequences clear for those students who deviated from the path, behavior in the school changed dramatically. Restoring a sense of physical safety was paramount before anything else could be addressed, including class attendance, academic performance, and teaching quality.

Similarly, Nancy Harris needed to demonstrate to patients and healthcare workers that they would be safe from government persecution if they came to her for treatment or chose to volunteer to be part of her effort. Throughout her years in Tibet she maintained that having relationships with the right people in power in China not only helped her to get things done, but also ensured, for the most part, a measure of stability, security, and continuity for the people around her.

Lily Yeh helped me understand that safety doesn't always mean physical safety; often, people's emotional and psychological wellbeing have to be considered before moving forward. Lily knew this when she gave the children at Dandelion School paints, paper, scissor, and brushes and asked them to create whatever they wanted. Then she asked them to talk to each other and express on paper what they heard. The personal stories were so raw that they could only have been shared from a safe place. Recognizing that those around you are coming from a similar state or a similar pain creates a sense that you are in this together. There is security in that.

Most people are surprised when they hear that Delancey Street has succeeded as a closed community of convicts and drug addicts without the support of outside experts, counselors, or security guards. Romero, one of the residents, believes it works because everyone who lives there is in it together. He remembers what it felt like when he first arrived from jail and how he saw some really bad guys he knew from prison. "And here they were doing well and walking around in ties," he said. "And they'd say, 'Just hang in there.'" He said that in the beginning, because he had to do everything with a small group comprised of newcomers, he felt he belonged to something, and in a sense that made him feel safe.

Heal Before You Rebuild

Mimi Silbert says that Romero lived at Delancey Street for two years before he smiled. It took that long for him to begin to heal. Then one day, while feasting at a banquet dinner where Mimi kept plying him with more and more food, he got the giggles. Then he started to laugh and couldn't stop. "I never laughed at myself before. I never knew how to or wanted to. But all of a sudden, instead of being balled up inside, I felt free," said Romero. Mimi says this is because when people first come to Delancey Street, they are like blocks of ice. It takes a long time to thaw, a long time to heal, after the lives they've led that got them there. But until that healing starts, not much else is going to change.

When Lily worked alongside the children and their parents in North Philadelphia, she felt their pain. As they created art together, they talked about what they had in common, the violence they had suffered, the family members lost, and the dissolution of hope. It was through the process of sharing that their healing began. Over time they transitioned from telling their stories to painting murals, converting vacant lots, planting gardens, and rebuilding homes.

Healing restores confidence and opens up pathways forward by acknowledging and working through what has been in the way. However, the concept of healing before rebuilding often involves more than working through personal pain and experience; sometimes it requires recommitting to forgotten values or tackling real life road blocks.

Devi Shetty had a promising career as a heart surgeon in London and then working for a wealthy family in Calcutta. But it was while caring for Mother Teresa that he was reminded of why he had chosen to be a doctor in the first place. Mother observed that he had a gift with children. She believed it was God's will that he save them.

Devi left Calcutta to return to his home state, intent on creating a way to deliver healthcare to everyone, not just those who could pay for it. In particular, he was focused on children. "We cannot afford to allow people to be in pain simply because they do not have money," he said. This became the moral foundation upon which he built everything else.

When Mechai Viravaidya was a young development economist travelling across rural Thailand, he noted that almost every family had at least ten children. He concluded that his country could not realize the benefits of economic development unless it curbed its exploding population. The ever-increasing mass of humanity put an insurmountable strain on the natural world and its resources. By making birth control widely available across Thailand, Mechai helped to slow birth rates and lay the foundation for the economic development which was to follow.

Ask People What They Need

Asking questions before devising a plan is perhaps the simplest, most effective approach to tackling problems. Yet those in government and large bureaucracies often neglect to do so. Why? Because they are paid to know the answer, and have what they believe is the experience and credentials to accomplish this. Thus, there is little incentive to solicit the input from those they are hired to help.

Under such conditions failure often follows. On the other hand, those who do ask questions often gain invaluable information that makes success much more likely.

Nancy couldn't secure or distribute enough vitamins and medicine to keep her malnourished and ailing patients alive. Thankfully, when she asked the elder Tibetans to share some of their old traditions for surviving she learned how for millennia mothers had exposed their babies to the sun and rubbed their bodies with oil every day in order to absorb necessary Vitamin D for growth and development. This provided Nancy with a home-grown solution to combatting rickets. She also learned by asking that it was impossible for a sick farmer to leave his work and travel a full day to the nearest medical clinic. This motivated her to build a network of health professionals and volunteers to reach hundreds of Tibet's remote villages.

From Jockin Arputham and Celine D'Cruz, I heard absurd stories of what happens when the powers-that-be forget to ask questions of those they are trying to help. Jockin tells the story of an agency that decided to plant trees in the slum to increase green space and make the community more "livable." Unfortunately, they had neglected to ask the slum dwellers what they wanted. Had they done so, they would have discovered that running water and working toilets were at the top of the list, not trees. They also would have realized that without that water, all those trees funded by generous donors were going to die.

Similarly, for years welfare agencies invested in health education, immunization, preventative care, nursery schools, and other programs to help the pavement dwellers. While these programs addressed individual problems that poor women faced, none got to the root of what kept them perpetually impoverished. When the NGO called SPARC asked the women what they really needed, they learned that the biggest obstacle to improving living conditions and livelihoods was the regular demolition of the huts by municipal crews. By asking the poor in the slums and on the pavement what they needed, SPARC was able to support a plan that made sense and could easily be executed as it engaged the people who knew the situation better than anyone else and had the most to gain from ensuring it was successful.

Mechai's Village Development Partnership is founded on the principle that the community must prioritize its needs and then articulate those priorities to potential funders. The effect of this, I discovered, is an empowered group of people who own the idea and feel personally responsible for seeing it through and repaying their loans.

By asking people what they need, two things happen: money and time are directed to those things that are most critical, and those who have identified the need become highly invested in ensuring that the solution succeeds and is sustainable. They become willing and valuable partners in the process.

Build a Community _____

By turning their individual struggles into a collective struggle the women on the pavement in Mumbai were able to accomplish what would have been impossible to do on their own. They found a solution to housing, started businesses with the support of their own savings fund, and transformed their lives and those of everyone around them forever. They were also instrumental in changing the way the city addresses urban infrastructure decisions and the allocation of resources.

The building of a community has played a key role in each of the other efforts as well. Delancey Street is a community of convicts and drug addicts who collectively rehabilitate each other. The Village of Arts and Humanities in North Philadelphia grew into a close community through the projects they worked on together with Lily. Participants learned and taught each other life skills and then took those to the surrounding neighborhoods to teach others.

Börje maintains that a school will not succeed in isolation. Rinkeby School survived and thrived because it was part of a greater community that incorporated the school, the town, social services, law enforcement, companies, universities, arts programs, and sports.

The work of the Terma Foundation helped to save over one million lives. The doctors and healthcare workers who devoted almost three decades to finding and treating patients did not succeed because each did the best job they could working in a government-run hospital or clinic. They succeeded because they were part of a larger community in Tibet that was committed to eradicating TB and curbing malnutrition beyond the scope of the national healthcare system.

Cultivate Connections and Alliances

Each of the efforts I have detailed in this book created a coalition of interested parties, stakeholders, partners, and investors. They did so in part because they lacked sufficient resources and needed others to help them get things done. More importantly, they saw what they were doing as part of a larger whole that had to function collectively for a long time. There were opportunities in these two-way relationships.

Börje was a master at orchestrating the cooperation and financial support of the various constituents that had interests in Rinkeby School. In doing so, he not only benefited his students, he also provided resources for the community to use and share. Devi's cooperation with the Indian Space Research Organization (ISRO) provided the technology that enabled him to consult with patients all over the world. At the same time, ISRO learned from the relationship and is now a major player in using space technology for the benefit of the greater society in India.

Jockin cultivated his relationships with people in government and in the nonprofit sector, as well as with community organizers across India and the world. His decision to form an alliance with SPARC, and have this well-respected organization play the role of "front office" while he and the slum dwellers wrote the plan for what should be done, was brilliant. The government and other agencies finally took the poor seriously instead of dismissing them as a nuisance.

Nancy, too, needed connections. She spoke often of the "grey area" and the importance of knowing what motivates your stakeholders to help you succeed. In a system as corrupt and malfunctioning as Tibet's, she had to cultivate relationships in villages, clinics, hospitals, government, military, and international agencies in order to survive.

Teach What You Learn and Create a Narrative _____

Mimi adopted the phrase "each one teach one" and built Delancey Street with the idea that every person has something to offer. When person A helps B, A gets better; when B helps C, B gets better, and so on. By helping someone else, you help yourself. By teaching someone else, you learn.

The most valuable assets each of these efforts had, even more than money, were the knowledge, the know-how, and the will of the individuals involved. During my travels I have seen time-and-again that the people whom we think we need to help are highly intelligent and creative, and quite capable of solving their own problems.

The women of Mahila Milan in Mumbai opened my eyes to this first. Though poor and illiterate, they were so wise. They figured out how to turn away the demolition teams, how to reclaim their belongings after they had been carted away, how to design affordable housing, and how to convince government to give them land for new homes. Every day they came together and shared with each other what they learned. They told and re-told their stories to create a narrative that became a virtual text book for their immediate community as well as other communities across India.

Incorporate Self-Sustainability Into the Solution _____

Mechai, Devi and Mimi each cautioned that work being done to change lives is too important to be at the mercy of fickle donors. Making what you do self-sustainable is critical for long-term survival. But it is not easy to do. Only three of the seven efforts are now financially self-sustaining. The revenue-generating parts of their work have also become an integral part of the solution.

Delancey Street's many businesses not only help to finance everyone's living expenses, they also allow residents to develop life and work skills to take with them when they leave.

The surgeries that Devi's team performs for-profit provide financing for the poor who cannot pay. The high capacity utilization at Narayana Health also serves to decrease its marginal costs. Diligently managing both sides of his profit and loss enables Devi to deliver affordable healthcare to everyone and still pay his bills.

Mechai created the Cabbages & Condoms restaurant to help finance his efforts to fight AIDS. Today most of the businesses under the umbrella of his organization are run by the rural poor for the benefit of their families, their communities, and the schools where they send their children.

Some of those I visited have not yet found ways to self-sustain financially. For now, they survive thanks to sweat equity, savings programs, donations in kind, and creative financing. For example, Jockin and the National Slum Dwellers Federation have been constructing low-cost housing in the slums, funded by the government, but designed and built by the slum dwellers. Rent income from these units funds the Federation's work. Nancy has prepared villagers and local doctors to carry forward without her. Through trial and error and hard work they have found ways to deliver healthcare which incorporates both traditional practices and the limited resources to which they had access. Because political instability cuts Tibet off from the rest of the world without notice, the solution to its health challenges has to be self-sustainable.

One Step at a Time, All the Time ————————————————

All environments are dynamic, every circumstance changes. Being able to weather the setbacks and roadblocks depends on how invested the players are in the process. When someone comes in with a plan that has proven successful elsewhere, funds and implements it, and then moves on, it does not create the ideal conditions for resiliency and resourcefulness. Similarly, when individual problems are targeted without addressing the root cause, the solutions are neither sustainable nor do they have far-reaching impact. By the time I arrived to meet each of these seven people, they had been on the ground working for a minimum of twenty-five years. Some had been at it for over forty years. When I asked them how they had kept at it for so long without becoming discouraged, every one of them said that they take each day as it comes, they take one step at a time.

I wanted to know then if they could envision an end to the work they were doing and what it would look like. Not one said that they could.

Mimi and Mechai were cultivating successors and Börje had already transitioned his role to another. But for the most part everyone saw that the ability to sustain and repeat what they had done to date would be in the hands of the people around them, those who now owned the process.

Nancy has started discussions with the Tibetans—asking them to take responsibility for the TB effort. Lily has transitioned out of every community in which she has worked. Devi's hospital has evolved into a health campus with specialties run by others who share his vision, Jockin's federation of slum dwellers continues to grow and add new members. In cities across the developing world communities continue to fight for legal empowerment and a seat at the table of urban development.

Mimi helped me understand that the work never ends, nor should it. As noted, she thinks we are on the edge of a revolution, but not the kind we think. In the future, she believes, wide-scale sustainable change will be brought about in a different way than what we have tried in the past. Making the world better does not happen by throwing money at solutions that work and then replicating them again and again in different places. She says: "Because if you understand the world, you know that when people find something that's world-class, they raise it up first and then tear it down later," People are impatient. They want the perfect answer and they want it now. But change that really matters takes a long-term committed effort and it happens one person at a time.

Return Of The Nightingales

In the fall of 2010, I went to Washington, D.C. to visit SPARC co-founder Celine D'Cruz, whom I hadn't seen since I was last in Mumbai. Celine was on loan to the World Bank for a project that involved UN Habitat, several local governments in Africa and Asia, and a handful of non-government organizations. Together they were exploring ways to work with cities in the developing world. Celine's role was to provide perspective from the community and street level. Her years of experience working in the slums of India and other countries made her a valuable asset to this team.

Though I followed the work of the World Bank from afar and had encountered several people who worked there, I had never visited its headquarters. When I went there to meet Celine, it was not what I expected. The institution was comprised of four individual buildings drawn together around a common atrium of glass and white metal that reached up thirteen stories. The structure consumed a full city block on Pennsylvania Avenue. It was much grander than I had imagined.

After passing through security, I joined a mass of professionals moving through the open spaces. The expressions on the faces around me communicated responsibility; there was energy in the words they used and urgency in their movements. I recognized several of the languages spoken.

The World Bank was originally created to help finance the reconstruction of Europe after two devastating wars. I suppose I had expected that it would reflect that legacy in some way—a dusty dark building filled with men in blue suits with the somber task of helping a decimated continent to survive. But it wasn't that at all. Instead it was a modern showcase, a suitable palace for a humanist king.

Although the World Bank is technically still a bank, its scope has broadened and its mission has changed. It now is comprised of five different organizations under one umbrella, and has effectively become, among other things, a development think-tank, a data repository, a publisher, an arbitrator of disputes, an insurance company, a financial advisor, a lender, and a donor. In the 1960s, it re-directed its focus from post-war reconstruction towards eradicating poverty and creating opportunity for people in the developing world. I have been told, however, that its progress with regard to these new goals has been underwhelming relative to the resources it has devoted to them. I don't know enough to judge that to be true, but as I looked at the impressive spread in front of me, I thought of Mechai and how much he had done in a much shorter period of time with about one hundred-billionth of the money.

As I made my way to find Celine in her office, I recalled the questions raised in our International Forums: Are organizations like the World Bank still capable of accomplishing what we have entrusted them to do for us? Could the resources be better used elsewhere? Should grassroots efforts like the ones I had encountered and small groups of committed individuals replace our large bureaucratic and expensive institutions in finding the solutions to the problems we face? Would they do a better job?

Celine pointed out that there are positive things that entities like the World Bank can do because of who they are. They can mobilize vast amounts of resources relatively quickly; they can influence policy that will enable more supportive environments for change within societies; they have the ability to create safe spaces for small groups to test new ideas and develop solutions that are relevant at the ground level. Most importantly, large institutions can do what Mimi Silbert described when she recounted what it meant to be a parent: they can support and encourage the small players, teach them and then connect them to the resources they need. The most effective role that these institutions can play is to be that "backboard"—the piece of wood behind the basketball net that helps the ball along. The backboard doesn't make the plays; but it supports those who do.

There is still a role for large institutions and governments to play in addressing the problems we face in our societies, but what is clear now is that grassroots and individuals should be playing a much bigger part than they have been. Large, broad-scale, well-funded solutions aren't necessarily the better ones. In fact, very often it is the small solution that prevails, the one that takes hold first because it makes the most sense and is easiest to implement. Sometimes a small solution is the only option; small might be all that there is time for. Small in many cases is better than big because it is nimble, closer to the problem, more in touch with the solution and can be adapted quickly when things change. And if there is one thing for certain—things will change.

A month after I left Börje Ehrstrand in Rinkeby, violence erupted on the streets again. While Nancy Harris was in California trying to get a visa to return to Tibet, more cases of TB were presented in the villages. Though life improved dramatically in the communities where Lily Yeh worked, residents still had to deal with crime and loss. While homelessness and poverty were addressed in one slum in India, circumstances changed in another and plunged a whole new group of people into hardship.

Challenges are a perpetual reality and part of the cycle of existence. Believing that there is a silver bullet to eradicate poverty forever is unrealistic. It will continue to exist because it is a relative state. While we may annihilate one disease, new ones will mutate. There is no end-game to solving problems; it is a continuous process.

Nancy said that the most effective model for dealing with challenges has more to do with the process than the answers. Adopting an approach that is flexible, innovative, and resourceful at adapting to change is better than locking onto an already formed, prescriptive and proven solution. The right answer now won't be the right answer next year. It is best to tackle the issues one step at a time. Individuals do this more effectively than large organizations.

Long before institutions were created to look after us, we helped one another to overcome illness, famine, homelessness, loss and violence. In fact, for millennia our survival as a species has depended on such cooperation. Communities formed and were bound by a common need and will to survive. It is only in the past one hundred years that we have expected large professional organizations and governments to do the job for us. In doing so, we have moved farther from the process ourselves.

In the early 20th century, the idea that government and institutions should take responsibility for those less fortunate took root in Western civilization. There was good reason for this. The emergence of a wealthy industrial class who built their fortunes on the backs of a growing underclass, followed by the Great Depression, brought a host of problems that were too great for the general population to deal with. While many individuals reached out to help, the challenge was too big and required an entity that could mobilize a large number of resources quickly. Thus, governments had to step in.

The Marshall Plan and the Point Four Program that followed ushered in an era of massive institutional foreign aid to needy countries in both the developed and developing world. What came from that was the most ambitious social crusade in human history; one where on a grand scale, those who had the best would save the rest, both at home and across the world. The paradigm that evolved—whether motivated by guilt, social justice, political power or other forces—was uniquely Western.

Knowingly and unknowingly, in our lifetime we have to a great degree abdicated our most fundamental of responsibilities as human beings to others and then convinced ourselves that those "others" are more capable of doing the job than we. In some ways we are like the nightingale in Hans Christian Anderson's story. We have given up our role to our gilded replacements: large aid organizations, charitable behemoths, social services and governments.

What will it take for each of us to reclaim the role we are meant to play in our communities and in the world? What was it that motivated the nightingale to return from the forest and help to save the man who had abandoned her in favor of her gold and jewel-encrusted replacement?

As a child I could not answer that question. But as an adult I have learned from people like Lily, Devi, Jockin, Nancy, Mechai, Börje and Mimi that each of us has the capacity to take back our responsibility for helping one other.

The story of the nightingale teaches that when you know how to make a difference for someone else, whether or not you are recognized or appreciated for it, you do it anyway.

In the beginning, I took this journey to find answers to big questions about the future of the world and the communities in which we live. But in time I realized I was also searching for the real heroes among us, the nightingales, the people who were doing small things that were making a big difference in the world. I wanted to know how it would feel to be one of them.

At first I expected that the people I sought would be larger-than-life, but instead I found them to be everyday people, with everyday problems and worries. They were mothers, fathers, estranged daughters, arrogant sons, alcoholics, high school dropouts, adulterers, and convicted criminals. They had experienced guilt, depression, anxiety, grief and failure, and, by their own admission, they had been dishonest, self-centered, misguided and lazy.

I thought I would be in awe of what they had done, for I could not imagine how ordinary people could accomplish what they had. Indeed, their persistence and courage was extraordinary. Yet, none possessed super-human skills. Each had simply applied his or her own talents and knowledge to solve a problem or address a need.

An artist who started building sculptures with neighborhood children in a vacant lot in North Philadelphia had ultimately helped empower a whole community. A young doctor had taught villagers what she knew about nutrition and hygiene through simple cartoons and demonstrations and saved hundreds of thousands of lives. A teacher had taken what he had learned from working with troubled students in a primarily school in an immigrant ghetto and turned around a high school rife with violence and truancy. An economist working on infrastructure projects in rural Thailand had traded a job in development for one in Planned Parenthood leading to successive programs to control population growth, fight AIDS, and create sustainable rural economic development. A promising young heart surgeon had decided to use the profits he made from his practice to provide medical care for the children of the poor.

The choices these individuals made helped me to see how any of us can make similar choices. We just need to believe that what we know how to do—paint, knit, write, cook, perform surgery, fix cars, grow vegetables, teach, run a business, build houses, train dogs, or virtually anything else—can be used for the benefit of someone else. Of course, to do something on the scale of what Nancy, Mimi, Devi, Mechai and others have done takes a commitment of many years. But a less ambitious effort is no less valuable if it helps to change a life, a community, or the world, for the better.

Digging where you are means seizing the opportunity right in front of you to make a difference, to make things better, to change bad situations into good. It means recognizing that any person is worth your help, not just those who are materially poor or visibly sick. Suffering, loss of dignity, physical pain, and emotional deprivation know no socioeconomic boundaries. The chance to make a meaningful difference in the world is right in front of us every day, wherever we live and whoever we are.

Digging where you are also means using what you've already got, what you already know, in order to help another. It doesn't mean you have to become someone you're not; it means re-discovering who you are and finding ways to share that with others. It also involves uncovering the assets in the people around you—what their talents are, who they know, what resources they have access to—so that they can help too.

What I have learned from the nightingales I have met in the world is that there is no right way to start digging where you are. Perhaps that is why there is so much promise in it. We are, all of us, surrounded by problems small and large, by individuals and communities in need of help. My hope is that like me, after meeting the people in this book, you will be inspired to view the world differently, and that if you see a way to do one small thing to change something for the better—you will do it.

Readings

Most of the material in this book is drawn from interviews and conversations I had with people over the past decade. Additional background comes from research and work conducted while developing programs for The International Forum. For my readers who would like to know more about the cultures, histories, issues, and people featured in this book I have included below a list of resources from my own library. It is by no means an exhaustive list but rather a place from which to start. The annotations provided are compiled from various published sources, book jackets and press releases.

The Alchemist _____

Bissinger, H. G. *A Prayer for the City*. New York: Random House, 1997.

This is an epic account of Philadelphia Mayor Ed Rendell, an utterly unique, unorthodox and idiosyncratic leader who will do anything to save his city; take unions head on, personally lobby President Clinton to save 10,000 defense jobs, or wrestle Smiley the Pig on Hot Dog Day—all the while bearing in mind the enteral fickleness of constituents whose favor may hinge on a missed garbage pick-up or an overzealous meter maid. It is also the story of citizens in crisis: a woman fighting ceaselessly to give her great-grandchildren a better life, a father of six who may lose his job at the Navy Shipyard, and a policy analyst whose experiences as a crime victim tempt her to abandon her job and ideals. A Prayer for the City describes a city on its knees (during the years when Lily Yeh was creating the Village of Arts and Humanities) and the rare combination of political courage and optimism that may be the only hope for America's urban centers.

Yeh, Lily. *Awakening Creativity: Dandelion School Blossoms*. Oakland, CA: New Village, 2011.

This book is Lily Yeh's own account of her experience with the students and teachers of the Dandelion School in Beijing, China. The pages are filled with her memories as well as photographs and reproductions of the art that was created.

The Healer

Chawla, Navin. *Mother Teresa: The Authorized Biography*. Rockport, MA: Element, 1996.

This is the story of Mother Teresa, re-told with great sensitivity and perception by a senior civil servant in the Government of India, who took up the cause of those affected by leprosy. In writing her biography, Chawla had Mother Teresa's full cooperation and involvement as well as access to her documents and letters. The book also incorporates input from her friends and helpers. This book was published before her death.

Collins, Larry, and Dominique Lapierre. *Freedom at Midnight*. New York: Simon and Schuster, 1975.

This is an account of the year 1947 and the events that culminated in the freedom of India from the British Raj. At the center of this drama are Nehru, Jinnah, Mountbatten and, of course, Gandhi, the gentle prophet of revolution, who stirred the masses of the most populous area on earth without raising his voice. It is an intimate account of the reasoning and events that led to the independence and division of India. To understand India today is to know from where it has come, particularly within the last century.

The Organizer

Arputham, J. "Developing New Approaches for People-Centred Development." *Environment and Urbanization* 20.2 (2008): 319-37.

This paper describes Jockin Arputham's life and work and the many different methods he used to fight eviction and get government support for people-centered development for over forty years beginning in the 1960s. It includes the long fight to protect Janata Colony in Mumbai and the formation of the National Slum Dwellers Federation in India. The text for this paper is drawn primarily from interviews conducted with Jockin during 2004 and 2005.

Hollick, Julian Crandall. *Apna Street*. Plymouth Meeting, PA: code-Mantra LLC. 2011.

Apna Street is the story of how a small group of pavement dwellers in Mumbai transformed their own lives and those of millions of other homeless people across India and the world. In 1986, pavement dwellers from several neighborhoods in Byculla came together to explore their dream of a secure home. This network of women's collectives named themselves Mahila Milan. Julian Crandall Hollick has recorded and produced radio documentaries about India for a quarter of a century. This book is drawn from his experience with the women in one of Mumbai's slums. It is available in digital form.

Mehta, Suketu. *Maximum City: Bombay Lost and Found.* New York: Alfred A. Knopf, 2004.

This is a portrait of Bombay and its people from an award-winning Indian-American fiction writer and journalist. It is an insider's view of this city. It takes us into the criminal underworld of rival Muslim and Hindu gangs who wrest control of the city's byzantine political and commercial systems, follows the life of a bar dancer who chose the only life available to her after a childhood of poverty and abuse, opens the doors onto the fantastic inner sanctums of Bollywood, and delves into the stories of the countless people who come from the villages in search of a better life and end up living on the sidewalks. Through his own experience living in the city, the author makes clear that Bombay—the world's largest city—is a harbinger of the vast megalopolises that will redefine the very idea of "the city" in the near future.

Sharma, Kalpana. *Rediscovering Dharavi: Stories from Asia's Largest Slum.* New Delhi: Penguin, 2000.

Spread over 175 hectares and swarming with one million people, Dharavi is often called "Asia's largest slum". But Dharavi is much more than a cold statistic. What makes it special are the extraordinary people who live there, many of whom have defied fate and an unhelpful State to prosper through a mix of backbreaking work, some luck, and a great deal of ingenuity. It is these men and women whom journalist Kalpana Sharma brings to life through a series of spellbinding stories. While recounting their tales, she also traces the history of Dharavi from the days when it was one of the six great fishing villages to the present times when it, along with other slums, is home to almost half of Mumbai.

The Warrior _____

Avendon, John F. *In Exile from the Land of the Snows – The Definitive Account of the Dalai Lama and Tibet Since the Chinese Conquest.* New York: Harper Perennial, 1997.

First published in 1986 and now considered a classic, here is an eloquent, engrossing account of the Dalai Lama's life in exile from Tibet, as revealed in interviews with the Dalai Lama, his friends, and followers

Iyer, Pico. *The Open Road – The Global Journey of the Fourteenth Dalai Lama.* New York: Vintage Departures, 2009.

For over three decades, Pico Iyer, one of the most cherished travel writers, has been a friend to the Dalai Lama. Over these years, through intimate conversations, he has come to know him in a way that few can claim. Here he paints an unprecedented portrait of one of the iconic figures of our time, explaining the Dalai Lama's work and ideas about politics, science, technology, and religion.

The Entrepreneur _____

D'Agnes, Thomas. *From Condoms to Cabbages: An Authorized Biography of Mechai Viravaidya.* Bangkok: Post Publishing Company, 2001.

This is a detailed account of the life and work of Mechai Viravaidya. It begins with his childhood and ends with his efforts in rural economic development. It recounts in detail the years he worked in family planning and his campaign to combat AIDS in Thailand. It is the story of a man who has committed his life to improving the well-being of his impoverished countrymen and women by helping them find the tools to lead healthy and productive lives.

Hayssen, Jonathan and Mechai Viravaidya. *Strategies to Strengthen NGO Capacity in Resource Mobilization Through Business Activities.* PDA and UNAIDS Joint Publication. 2001.

The work of non-governmental organizations (NGOs) is by nature unprofitable. Traditionally, they have relied on the goodwill and generosity of others to cover the costs of their activities through grants and donations. When the costs of an NGO's core activities exceed its revenues, it is forced to either reduce the quantity and/or quality of its work, or to find new sources of funds to cover the difference. Reaching out to new donors with innovative fund-raising approaches is usually the first step. Redesigning program activities to include cost recovery components, whereby the beneficiaries or clients of the NGO pay part of program costs, is a second approach. A third alternative is for the NGO to make money through commercial ventures. This paper discusses alternative sources of funding for NGOs with special attention to commercial activities as a solution. This document can be accessed on line at http://pdf.usaid.gov/pdf_docs/pnadb694.pdf

Prahalad, C. K. *The Fortune at the Bottom of the Pyramid: Eradicating Poverty through Profits.* Upper Saddle River, NJ: Wharton School Pub., 2010.

In this book the author makes the case that the typical pictures of poverty mask the fact that the very poor represent resilient entrepreneurs and value-conscious consumers. What is needed is a better approach to help the poor achieve sustainable, win-win scenarios where they are actively engaged and, at the same time, the companies providing products and services to them are profitable. The book illustrates how this might be possible with the help of case studies of business successes from the bottom of the pyramid.

The Team

Dahlin, Bo. "From The Worst To The First: The Story Of The Rinkeby School." *Bildung Und Erziehung* 63.3. 2010.

The author is a professor of Education at Karlstad University in Sweden. This paper outlines some of the elements of the turn-around of Rinkeby School in the period between 1989 and 2007 that led to the successful transformation of Rinkeby School.

Tough, Paul. *Whatever it Takes*, New York: First Mariner Books, 2009.

What would it take to change the lives of poor children—not one by one, through heroic interventions and occasional miracles, but in big numbers, and in a way that could be replicated nationwide? This is the question that led Geoffrey Canada to create the Harlem Children's Zone, a ninety-seven-block laboratory in central Harlem where he tested new and sometimes controversial ideas about poverty in America. His conclusion: if you want poor kids to be able to compete with their middle-class peers, you need to change everything in their lives—their schools, their neighborhoods, even the child-rearing practices of their parents. This book is a portrait not only of Geoffrey Canada but of the parents and children in Harlem who are struggling to better their lives, often against great odds.

The Inmate _____

Bernstein, Nell. *Burning Down the House: The End of Juvenile Prison.* New York: The New Press, 2014.

This book focuses on the juvenile justice system and argues that there is simply no good way to lock up a child. Making the radical argument that state-run detention centers should be abolished completely, the author points out that our system of juvenile justice flies in the face of everything we know about what motivates young people to change. The author's portraits of young people, abused by the system intended to protect and rehabilitate them, are interwoven with reporting on innovative programs that provide effective alternatives to putting children behind bars.

Dig Where You Are _____

Bornstein, David. *How to Change the World: Social Entrepreneurs and the Power of New Ideas.* Oxford: Oxford University Press, 2004.

This book is about people who have both changed their lives and found ways to change the world. It tells of people who have discovered how to use their talents and energy to advance meaningful change — defiant people who refuse to accept the status quo, who simply cannot sit still in the face of injustice, suffering, or wastefulness. The book shows how innovators advance new models to solve social and economic problems — how they make headway against the odds. This book is for individuals who seek to understand the fast growing field of "social entrepreneurship" and discover opportunities to enrich their work and their lives.

Easterly, William. *The White Man's Burden: Why the West's Efforts to Aid the Rest Have Done so Much Ill and So Little Good.* New York: Penguin, 2006.

This book explores why Western aid has failed to reach and help the world's most desperate poor. It argues why the West must face its own history of ineptitude and hold its aid agencies accountable for the results of their actions. Most importantly the author makes the case for why the focus on having the right plan to solve the problem is a misdirected approach, while having no plan at all is the better path. "Planners" most often fail in spite of their good intentions and well formed solutions, while "searchers" succeed explicitly because they do not have the answers. Why? (The White Man's Burden is particularly helpful in providing a broader historical and social context for why the people of *Dig Where You Are* have succeeded where others have not).

Kretzmann, John P. and John L. McNight. *Building Communities from the Inside Out: A Path Toward Finding and Mobilizing a Community's Assets.* Chicago: ACTA Publications, 1993.

Across the United States, communities are in trouble. But everywhere, creative local leaders are fighting back, rebuilding neighborhoods and communities. And they are succeeding by starting with what they already have. In the face of diminished prospects for outside help, they are turning to their neighbors and to the local citizen associations and institutions that lie at the heart of their community. This guide summarizes lessons learned by studying successful community-building initiatives in hundreds of neighborhoods across the United States. It outlines in simple, "neighborhood-friendly" terms, what local communities can do to start their own journeys down the path of asset-based development. This guide will be helpful to local community leaders, leaders of local associations and institutions, government officials, and leaders in the philanthropic and business communities who wish to support effective community-building strategies.

Kristof, Nicholas D., and Sheryl WuDunn. *A Path Appears: Enriching the Lives of Others—and Ourselves.* New York: Alfred A. Knopf, 2014.

A Path Appears is a tapestry of people who are making the world a better place and a guide to the ways that we can do the same— whether with a donation, with our time, by capitalizing on our skills as individuals, or by using the resources of our businesses. The authors identify successful local and global initiatives, and share astonishing stories from the front lines of social progress. We see the compelling, inspiring truth of how real people have changed the world, upending the idea that one person can't make a difference. This book provides results-driven advice on how each of us can effectively give and reveals the lasting benefits we gain in return.

Soto, Hernando de. *The Mystery of Capital: Why Capitalism Triumphs in the West and Fails Everywhere Else.* New York: Basic, 2000.

Charitable organizations have so emphasized the miseries and helplessness of the world's poor that no one has properly documented their capacity for accumulating assets—writes de Soto. In this book, the author takes up the question: Why do some countries succeed at capitalism while others fail? Contrary to the popular view that success is determined by cultural differences, de Soto finds that it actually has everything to do with the legal structure of property and property rights. Every developed nation in the world at one time went through the transformation from predominantly informal, extralegal ownership to a formal, unified legal property system. In the West we've forgotten that creating this system is also what allowed people everywhere to leverage property into wealth. (This book is particularly helpful in providing context for the success of both Mechai's and Jockin's work with the urban and rural poor.)

Web Sites _____

Barefoot Artists. *barefootartists.org*

Narayana Health. *narayanahealth.org*

National Slum Dwellers Federation. *sparcindia.org/aboutnsdf.php*

Slum Dwellers International. *sdinet.org*

Terma Foundation. *terma.org*

Population and Community Development Association. *pda.or.th*

Rinkeby School. *rinkebyskolan.stockholm.se*

Delancey Street Foundation. *delanceystreetfoundation.org*

In Appreciation

I am eternally grateful to Lily Yeh, Devi Shetty, Jockin Arputham, Nancy Harris, Börje Ehrstrand, Mechai Viravaidya, and Mimi Silbert, without whom there would be no Dig Where You Are. These remarkable individuals invited me into their homes, their places of work, and their communities, and took the time to share with me their stories. In the course of re-connecting with each of them, I expected at least once to be put off given how busy they are, but I never was. In fact, just the opposite – I was fed, I was given a place to sleep, a drive to where I was going, a scarf to keep me warm, and in every case an invitation to return. Because of their generosity of time – their stories can now be shared. If even one person is inspired to dig where they are because of what they read here, we will have succeeded.

During the time I spent with the men and women in this book I learned much about their lives and the choices they have made. Some spoke of the darker sides of their journey, the trade-offs and sacrifices, and the relationships that suffered because of the all-out commitment they had to give to their work. I have divulged very few of these details out of respect for their privacy. However because they were open and willing to share so much of themselves with me, I was able to, with confidence, tell the stories of how "real" people, not super-humans, can change the world.

To realize this project from idea to published book it took a small group of caring and committed individuals. I am grateful to those who in the beginning helped me to find, or who introduced me to, some of the people about whom I write. Thank you to John

Abrahamson, Rajat Banerji, Peggy Day, Sheela Patel, Ramesh and Swati Ramanathan, and Lindsey Carver Schortz. Thank you to Rupali and Gaurav Bhatia in India and Derong Chen in China for their hospitality and support during my many weeks on the road and away from home.

To my editors Steve and Sharon Fiffer, to whom I presented the idea of this book in 2008, who have supported and believed in the project ever since—I am so grateful. You helped me to find my voice and stuck with me through the toughest parts. Thank you as well to my fellow writers in the Wesley Workshop. To SPARC Mumbai, Terma Foundation and Laila Bakken for sharing photographs of Jockin Arputham, Nancy Harris and Börje Ehrstrand respectively and to Mary Lou Bouley for your help in cataloguing– thank you. It takes a community to make a book become a reality and you are my community.

I am deeply grateful to my parents who pushed me out into the world at an early age so that I would learn from others who were different than I, while also understanding the importance of seeing things from other perspectives. To my mother who has always encouraged me to explore the unfamiliar corners of the world; to my father who charged me with running The International Forum when I was only 37 years old. It was this that set me on a path to meet these extraordinary people. I am thankful in particular for my father's support when I decided to write this book. As the only other person who has met and knows each of these people, his thoughtful reflections and insight into their stories has been an invaluable asset in the creation of this work. Furthermore his insistence that I finish it so others could read it brought closure to a journey which took much longer than anticipated.

To Celine D'Cruz, with whom I shared the idea of this project before it became reality, who has become not only my dear friend, but also my sounding board and teacher, I am grateful for her help in building my understanding of the on-the-ground issues and opportunities we face in the world today and the power of communities to solve them.

To Zygmunt Nagorski who inspired me to follow my dream no matter how unformed it seemed at first and then to see it through. He challenged me to listen to the call when it came, to tell the stories that had been told to me, to stand up for what I believed in, to be obstinate enough to do what I thought made sense with my life. I have written this book in memory of him.

Finally to my husband Brian, who with patience and understanding continues to encourage me to dig where I am. Without his support none of this would have been possible.

Author Biography

Nan Alexander Doyal has lived and worked in North America, Europe and Asia for more than three decades, most recently as President of The International Forum – an organization that designs active learning experiences for the leaders of global corporations. For more than ten years she worked together with a team around the world to design and lead travelling forums across Japan, China, India, Thailand, Poland, Czech Republic, Sweden, Belgium and the United States. These experiences combined face-to-face conversations with active learning encounters and visits to companies, schools, hospitals and other organizations to meet with leaders and individuals engaged in solving problems and creating opportunity. Executives from over 250 companies and 15 countries have participated in The International Forum since it was founded in 1988 at The Wharton School. Prior to joining The International Forum she was a vice president with Ameritech Corporation in Chicago, Illinois, ran her own direct marketing firm, held several positions at American Express Travel Related Services Co. Inc. in New York, worked for Shiseido Co. Ltd. in Tokyo, Japan and for RBC Dominion Securities, in Toronto, Canada. She is a graduate of Smith College and The Wharton School, University of Pennsylvania. *Dig Where You Are* is her first book.